THE POWER OF
ADAPTATION

A GUIDE TO BOTTOM-UP GROWTH THAT LASTS

LUCA DELLANNA

Luca Dellanna

@DellAnnaLuca
Luca-dellanna.com

First edition
March 2024 update

CONTENTS

APPENDIX

INTRODUCTION

The last words my father said to me on his deathbed were, "Everything changes."

Indeed, the world changes. And it is up to us to change ourselves so that we keep up to speed. Otherwise, we will be left behind.

In this book, I will show you how to adapt to the environment while remaining true to yourself. This book can apply both to people (you) and organizations (your company, your social group, etc.). It follows the principles I learned in my personal and professional life, which brought me from being a shy teenager who couldn't speak for himself to leading large teams, getting a job in a Fortune 100 before graduating, quitting the corporate world at 26 years old, and achieving a happy and fulfilling life.

Natural selection

Natural selection has been the key driver for adaptation since ever.

In appearance, it is a cruel process: the unfit die. However, we humans can adapt much faster than any other species. Therefore, we have a choice: not adapting and be on the bad side of natural selection, or using natural selection on our own mental patterns to drive our personal growth and be on the good side of natural selection. We either have to play with natural selection or be played by it.

In this book, I will teach you how to play with natural selection and how to harness its power to grow yourself or your organization.

Bottom-up change

Many books on personal or organizational change provide advice that is top-down and is subject to survivorship bias: these often sound good in theory but fail when put into practice. Instead, the focus of this book is bottom-up change, the only type of change that produces enduring results.

The footnotes and the appendix

In the footnotes and the appendix, you will find not only references but also justifications for what has been written in the corpus of the text or interesting facts and considerations that can increase the understanding of the subject.

I really suggest reading them.

Questions?

You can reach me at **Luca@Luca-dellanna.com**

A selection of the key responses will be republished on my website, **Luca-dellanna.com**

"Change is inevitable,

*but you can influence whether it happens **within** you or **upon** you."*

"Much of Antifragility is about pulling change forward in time, so that you change before it's too painful, and pushing it down, so that it happens within you instead of upon you."

PART I

PRINCIPLES

In Part 1, I will explore the necessity of adaptation at both the individual and the organizational level, going deeper into its processes and how to achieve it effectively.

With this understanding in place, in Part 2, I will propose a practical 4-step process you can use to build bottom-up, self-directed personal growth that is long-lasting.

1

A FAUSTIAN BARGAIN

Natural selection is amazing. Thanks to it, animal species obtained abilities that, if bestowed to us, would be deemed "superpowers." Some of these include the power of flight (most winged animals), the power of invisibility (chameleons), the power of shapeshifting (mimic octopuses), the power of sensing (bats), and even the power of survival in sidereal space (tardigrades[1]).

However, **the true value of natural selection**[2] does not lie in its ability to grant a species a specific "superpower"; it **lies in its ability to provide all species with any adaptation they might need to survive.** If the climate gets colder, the next generations will grow bigger fur. If a new predator arrives, the next generations will develop mutations to improve their chances of fighting or evading it. No matter how the environment changes and no matter how threats adapt, natural selection provides all species with the exact tools they need.[3]

The capacity for adaptation is the most important asset of any species and the source of all its other "superpowers."[4] However, it comes at a cost.

Fitness

Before exploring the costs that we have to pay in exchange for our capacity to adapt, it is crucial first to define what it means to be fit in the context of adaptation.

Fitness is the ability to survive the environment.[5] Some authors define fitness as the ability to thrive; however, this is a rather short-term definition. In the long term, only the ability to survive (and to reproduce) matters. If you want any proof, ask any dinosaur. Except you can't, because they thrived in the Mesozoic era but did not survive it. Apparently, they weren't so fit, after all.[6]

Great powers come with great costs

The power of adaptation comes at a cost. In order for an animal species to develop longer legs, for example, those with shorter ones have to die.[7] **The fitness of a species improves when the unfit within its population die.**

(Just to be clear: I am in no way saying that the unfit should get "selected out"; the opposite, I condemn it. With this book, I try to provide a roadmap for an alternative that allows the unfit to avoid getting harmed by natural selection. This will be explained progressively during the book.)

Imagine a group of giraffes (fun fact: a group of giraffes is called a *tower*[8]). Each giraffe is, on average, 5 meters tall. Not all giraffes in the tower have the same height: some might be 4.9 meters tall, most of them might be 5 meters tall, and some are 5.1 meters tall.

Parents produce offspring that are similar to them, with some slight random variation. Let's assume that each female giraffe produces offspring that, at adulthood, will be as tall as their parent, with a standard deviation of plus or minus 0.1 meters. Consider, for example, a female giraffe who is 5.1 meters tall with four children. Each would grow to a height that is similar to hers but with some slight variations: one is 5 meters tall, two are 5.1 meters tall, and one is 5.2 meters tall. Similarly, a giraffe who is 4.9 meters tall might have offspring whose height ranges between 4.8 and 5.0 meters. (Refer to the figure below).

(This is a simplified example of how reproduction works; for full details and its assumptions, follow the footnote[9].)

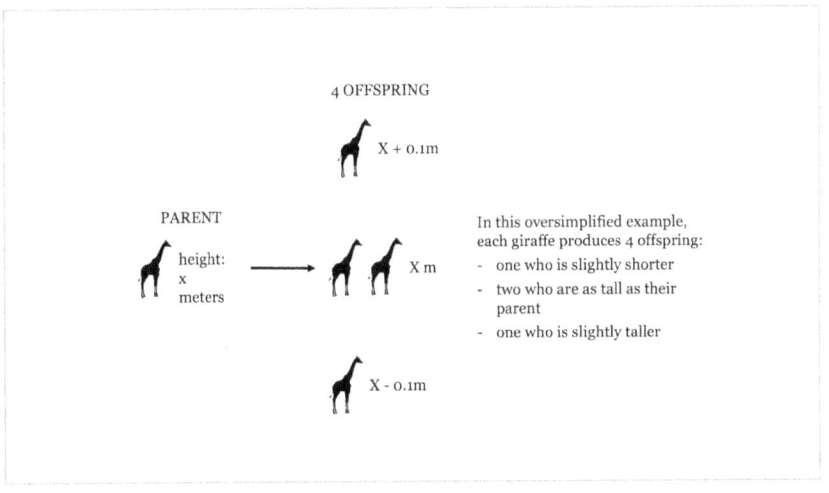

4 OFFSPRING

X + 0.1m

PARENT

height:
x
meters

X m

X - 0.1m

In this oversimplified example, each giraffe produces 4 offspring:
- one who is slightly shorter
- two who are as tall as their parent
- one who is slightly taller

Now, imagine that, suddenly, all trees grew taller,[10] and only the giraffes who are at least 5.1 meters tall can reach the leaves and feed themselves. The giraffes who are 4.9- and 5.0-meters tall would die, and only the giraffes who are 5.1-meters tall would be left to reproduce. All the offspring would, therefore, have their height comprised between 5.0 and 5.2 meters, and the average height would then increase to about 5.1 meters. **The death of the unfit** – those who were too short – **caused an evolution in the opposite direction** to their relative phenotype (the short dying caused the population to become their opposite: taller. The death of the short giraffes results in an increase in the average height of the remaining sample: the second generation is thus taller[11]). See the following picture.

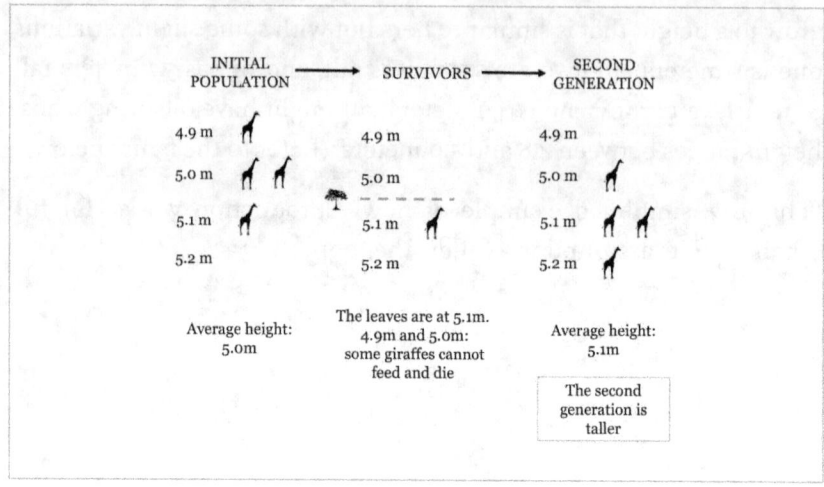

Let's consider an alternative scenario, in which the tall giraffes are exceptionally kind and spend part of their time cutting leaves from the tall trees to give them to those who cannot reach them. In this scenario, all giraffes survive and reproduce. The new population will have a height comprised between 4.8 and 5.2 meters; their average height will be 5.0 meters, the same as their parents. **No death, no evolution.**

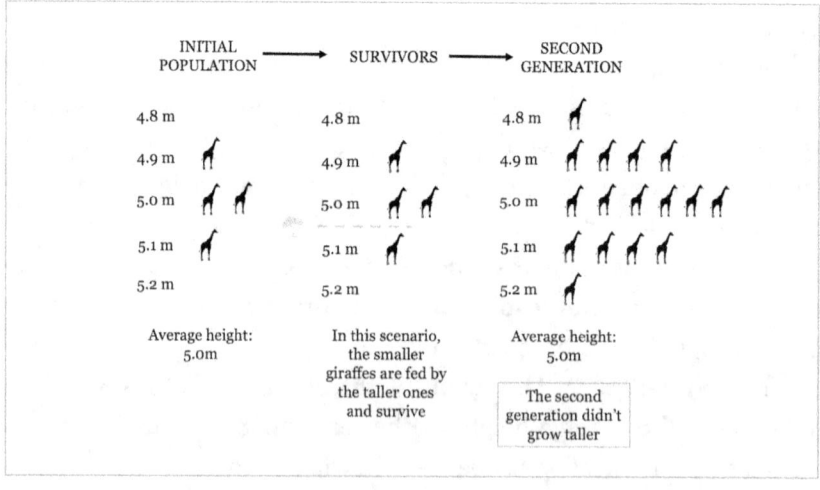

Since all members of the species survive, this scenario could be seen as more favorable than the first one. However, this is better **only if the environment is stable.** If the trees are forever 5.1 meters tall, then sure, the tallest giraffes can keep feeding their shorter siblings. However, the trees will likely keep growing[12] to the point where only a giraffe, which is 5.2 meters tall, can grab its leaves, at which point the group of giraffes in the second scenario will find themselves in a tough spot. Almost none of them will be able to reach the leaves, and the very few who will, will not be able to feed the entire group.[13] Conversely, a higher *proportion* of the giraffes in the first scenario will be able to survive by feeding themselves from the tall trees: they evolved for that.

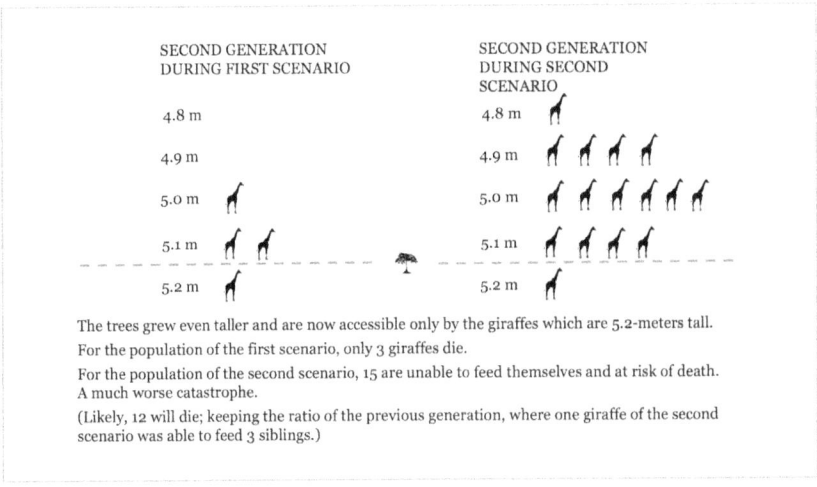

SECOND GENERATION
DURING FIRST SCENARIO

SECOND GENERATION
DURING SECOND
SCENARIO

4.8 m

4.9 m

5.0 m

5.1 m

5.2 m

The trees grew even taller and are now accessible only by the giraffes which are 5.2-meters tall.
For the population of the first scenario, only 3 giraffes die.
For the population of the second scenario, 15 are unable to feed themselves and at risk of death. A much worse catastrophe.
(Likely, 12 will die; keeping the ratio of the previous generation, where one giraffe of the second scenario was able to feed 3 siblings.)

Summing it up: for adaptation to take place, the unfit must die. Or, highlighting the cause-effect relationship: **it is the death of the unfit that causes adaptation** in the species.

This might seem a rather grim picture. However, the reality is much brighter: as the following chapter shows, we can harness the power of adaptation to avoid death and thrive instead.

1. Microscopic, eight-legged, half-a-centimeter-long "water bears," with individual species able to survive extreme conditions that would be rapidly fatal to all other known life forms, such as exposure to extreme temperatures, extreme pressures (both high and low), air deprivation, radiation, dehydration, and starvation.

2. Natural selection is only one of two adaptation processes that species use to improve their fitness in an everchanging environment; the second is *calibration*. Readers can find an essay detailing the latter in the appendix.

3. Provided those changes are slow and progressive enough. This point will be explored in a chapter further down in this book.

4. Adaptation is so important that any living species has it; otherwise, it would have been extinct or, most probably, would not have seen the light at all.

5. ...and to reproduce. However, this book is intended as a guide for survival, not for reproduction; therefore, reproduction will be ignored.

6. Some might object that dinosaurs died because the environment suddenly changed. Well, it is a matter of the temporal scope of the environment. Sure, the short-term environment did change. However, one could argue that it is not improbable that a meteor would strike the Earth every few hundred million years and that the dinosaurs evolved to a subset of the environment that assumed no meteorite strike. Very unfit species die immediately; unfit species thrive in the current environment (e.g., the dinosaurs); very fit species thrive over the long term, no matter the environment (e.g., those species that survived the meteorite event). This point might seem absurd now, but it will be repeated more clearly and practically in a later chapter.

7. Or being prevented from reproducing.

8. Other interesting animal collective nouns include a parliament of owls, a glaring of cats, a rhumba of rattlesnakes, an army of caterpillars, and a congregation of alligators.

9. This simplified example of reproduction has been used to facilitate clarity & ease of understanding to demonstrate how natural selection affects evolution. In reality, reproduction is much more complex. For example, females make a variable number of offspring, the offspring inherit both the DNA of the male parent and of the female one, only a few dominant males get to reproduce, and so on. Moreover, I am considering only the hypothesis that giraffes evolved a long neck to reach food at heights and not for fighting. This example is not about giraffes but about showing how evolution works.

10. Why would they do that? Well, because taller trees get eaten less and therefore survive and reproduce more.

11. The image of the tree in this series of charts has been drawn by deviantart.com/sepandj.

12. Why would the trees keep growing? Because the shorter trees get eaten, and only the taller ones get to reproduce. Trees and giraffes are in competitive evolution.

13. In the hypothesis of an initial distribution of 25% of giraffes 4.9 meters tall, 50% 5.0 meters tall, and 25% 5.1 meters tall, and assuming that each giraffe makes 4 children (one who is 0.1 meters shorter, one who is 0.1 meters taller, and two who are of the same height), after one generation, 25% of the giraffes will be 5.2 meters tall in the first scenario and only 6.25% will in the second scenario.

    In the first scenario, therefore, three giraffes do not survive the first selection, and three more do not survive the second (6 deaths total). Assuming that one kind and tall giraffe can feed three siblings, no giraffes die in the first scenario, but 12 die in the second one (12 deaths total). It almost looks like the act of kindness caused the death of 6 more giraffes. (Of course, it is an exaggerated example; in reality, the conditions would have changed much more slowly; at a certain point, some giraffes would have to die, and evolution would have started taking place.)

    Throughout this book, I will introduce the concept that kindness must be evaluated over the long term and considering second-order effects (i.e., how populations adapt to the act of kindness and how the environment itself adapts).

2

ADAPT OR PERISH

Before brightening the situation with a solution that does not involve humans left behind for humanity to adapt effectively, let me clarify a key point.

We cannot opt out of natural selection. We cannot renounce the superpower of adaptation (and its costs) in exchange for leaving the unfit unscathed.

As in the giraffes' example above, **the suffering of the unfit can only be delayed.** (Of course, this does not mean that the unfit cannot, or should not, be helped to become fitter so that they can themselves become more resistant to adversities. Nor does it mean that those who cannot adapt shouldn't be supported. But the large part of the population that can adapt, should.)

Furthermore, **denying the need for adaptation exacerbates the fitness gap between a population and an everchanging environment;** trying to close this gap by any means other than adaptation is a game lost in advance. (As I will explain later, all solutions must be bottom-up also to be long-term – hence, the importance of bottom-up adaptation, the topic of this book.)

Going back to the example involving giraffes, if the individuals who are tall enough to reach the leaves were to feed those who are shorter, no short giraffe would die. Therefore, the population would not evolve towards being taller. However, if the plants keep becoming taller,[1] the giraffe population would suffer a famine: now, almost no giraffe is able to reach any leaf because, as a species, they did not adapt to the environment, and the fitness gap between the average of the population and what is required by the environment kept growing.

Deciding not to adapt is like taking a debt. We gain immediate comfort but increase the gap between who we are and who we need to be in order to survive the environment. Eventually, we will have to catch up with the environment; the alternative is being wiped out.

Denying the necessity of adaptation is akin to refusing to repay a debt – this is not the debtor's call, but the creditor's. In the case of adaptation, the creditor is the environment, and the environment always collects its debts.

––––––

To address some ethical concerns: I do not deny that some people or populations "got luckier" and started in a better position than others; nevertheless, everyone has a personal responsibility to adapt as much as possible, where "as much as possible" is a function of each situation at a given point of time; I clarify this concept in the appendix. In the second part of this book, "Personal Growth," I explain why personal adaptation is everyone's responsibility.

––––––

Bad employees: to keep, or to fire?

Now, let's explore how environmental changes and adaptation can impact us at an organizational level. Take, for example, a company with a few employees who are not doing a good job. Perhaps these are employees whose skills were relevant in the past but who were unable to learn new skills that are more relevant to an evolving job market. Or they might simply be employees whose skills were never good enough to start with and who have not been able to improve them. In both instances, their contribution to the company is subpar.

The company has two choices: keeping these employees or firing them. If the company keeps them, the average employee contribution will be low. This lowers the competitiveness of the company, in turn leading to less business, causing revenues and profits to plummet, up to the point where layoffs become no longer a choice but a necessity. In the worst case, the company might be forced to close. In this scenario, everyone loses (both the better-performing employees and the less-performing ones).[2]

Instead, by firing its poorest-performing employees, a company can increase the average performance of its employees (its fitness) and, therefore, its competitiveness, its business, and its profits, up to the point in which it will be able to grow bigger and hire more employees than it laid off. Of course, this is very bad for the employees who got fired, and this is why, in the next section, I suggest a third alternative, which allows the company to adapt while retaining most of its employees. Before, let me repeat the point of this section:

If the environment permanently drifts in a direction, adaptation is not a choice but a necessity. Resisting it will cause everyone (both the fit and the unfit) to suffer.

Status quo

Having to decide between keeping and firing can be difficult. As such, many companies react to the situation in the example by keeping the status quo, crossing their fingers & hoping for the best. "Surely," they think, "the hard times are only temporary; if we survive a few months more, the business will improve, and we will have enough money to keep all our employees, even those who underperform." Unfortunately, this is almost never the case.

Take a sinking ship, for example. If the underlying issue has been identified as having holes in its structure, it is crucial to fix them. Using buckets to throw water out of the ship will alleviate the flooding but will not prevent the ship from sinking. If the holes remain unfixed, when a thunderstorm comes, the tides will flood the ship; no matter how fast the crew scoops the water out of it, it will become severely flooded and eventually sink.

If the root problem is not solved, it will keep generating new problems. Each individual problem is temporary, but the flux of problems generated by the root one is permanent.

The alternative

Between keeping or firing underperforming employees, the management of the company from the previous example can exercise a third option: making them adapt.

Employees are humans, and humans are an ensemble of habits and beliefs. Some of these habits and beliefs have a positive effect on their ability to perform well at their job, while others have a negative effect. If the manager can break the habits and change the beliefs dampening productivity, then the employees will become more productive, thus removing the need to fire them because they were underperforming.

For example, the manager might constantly reprimand the employee who poorly performs a given task because of a counterproductive habit of his (such as lack of planning or tendency to procrastinate) until it has eliminated this behavior and caused the employee to adapt (by adopting the necessary behavior).[3]

In an ever-changing world, **adaptation is a necessity; however, we can choose the level at which it takes place.**

A group of people can adapt by letting natural selection kill* its unfit members, or by letting natural selection kill* the unfit behaviors of its unfit members.

(*) To "kill" refers here to any action that causes a member of the population to exit that population. For example, being fired, being expelled, being socially emarginated, going bankrupt, and so on.

As a general rule, the more the need for adaptation is pushed towards a lower layer, the less suffering will be caused over the long term. If the employees adapt, they will perhaps have to suffer slightly during the adaptation, but they will never have to suffer from being unemployed. If a person adapts, he or she might suffer slightly during the adaptation period but will never have to suffer from being socially or economically emarginated.[4]

Some may consider the killing of habits and beliefs a harsh reality. However, if the environment in which a person lives (or works) changes, then that person will have to change as well, because the population he is part of (his friends and his colleagues) will either change (in which case he will be left behind) or will not change (in which case, the whole group will be left behind); neither scenario is appealing.

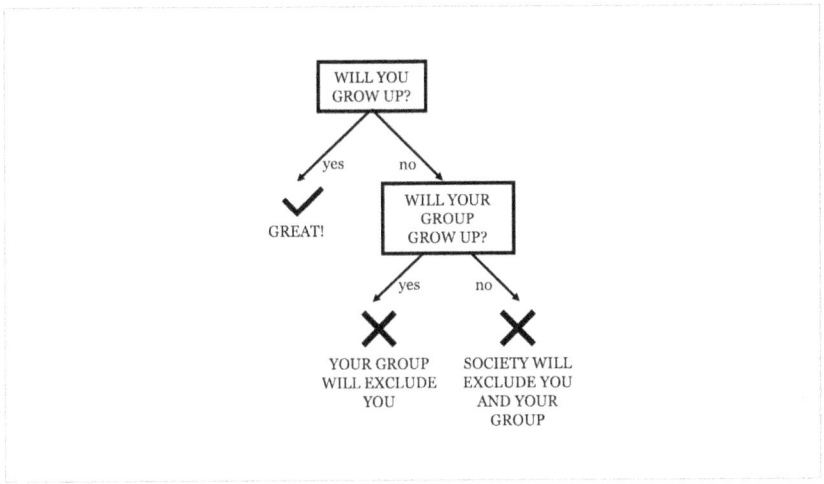

Take the example of a kid in his early teens. Given the environment he lives in, he can spend his time doing what teenagers do and do great. When he becomes twenty-something, he must grow up and become more mature. Let's say he doesn't. He will still probably have a good life and enjoy spending time with his friends who did not grow up either. But things might change soon.

When he gets closer to his thirties, if he doesn't grow up and mature yet, two scenarios will unfold. Either his friends grow up and exclude him from his group, or his friends do not grow up and keep him in the group. However, in the latter case, now it is the broader society that will exclude the whole group – those who have not grown up yet in their thirties generally enjoy a frustrating subpar life without much money, good jobs, good partners, and good physical health. Neither scenario looks good for the kid who did not want to grow up.

The solution, of course, is to grow up – to adapt.

Overpreservation leads to destruction

Alan is a man in his forties who enjoys writing in his free time. Over the last few years, he wrote a few chapters of a book and sent it to some friends. Some told him that his stories are interesting, even if they do not really believe so. Others told him that the main character, Boris, is quite boring. However, Alan is emotionally attached to Boris and does not want to change him: after all, it was the first character he ever put on ink. Over time, to protect Boris, Alan stopped sending drafts to the friends of his who gave him real advice and only showed them to his acquaintances who gave him sugarcoated comments. Last summer, Alan submitted his book to 5 publishers. They all rejected his proposal, criticizing his writing and his representation of the main character. Morally broken, Alan resigned to abandon his dream of becoming a writer.

To protect every single piece of his identity as a writer, including every single facet of his pet character, Alan ended up having to quit his dream to become a writer. His writing was not good enough: it needed to adapt. His characters were not good enough: they needed to adapt. **By striving to preserve all of them, he ended up killing them all.** Had Alan instead kept some of Boris' traits but changed others in order to make him more interesting, Boris would still be alive. Had Alan accepted that some elements of his writing style were flawed and had to be replaced, his writing style would have adapted, and he would not have had to quit his literary dreams.

When we are not good enough, we have the option to try to understand which part of us is not good enough, let it go, and replace it with a better one. If we do not do that, people for whom we are not good enough might have to let us go and replace us with someone better. I'm not discussing if it is fair for them to do it, or if it is right for us to change parts of ourselves that we like; I'm just pointing out a potential consequence that might happen if we do not. Similarly, I am not advising that we change every single part of us at the whim of any piece of feedback; in the second part of this book, I will teach you how to distinguish between which pieces of feedback should be listened to and which ones should not.

Chapter summary

- In an ever-changing world, adaptation is a necessity; however, we can choose the level at which it takes place.

- A group of people can adapt by letting natural selection kill its unfit members or by letting natural selection "kill" the unfit behaviors of its unfit members.

- Similarly, a person can adapt by letting natural selection "kill" his or her unfit mental patterns. If instead he or she hangs on them, (s)he puts him or herself at risk instead.

In the next chapter

In the next chapter, we will explore the three ways in which adaptation can take place.

---

1. This assumption is key. As I will explain later, a population providing for the needs of the unfit is beneficial only if the "unfitness" is temporary due to an exceptional change in the environment that is expected to revert soon to the previous condition. These situations are extremely rare in nature. More often, the environment is undergoing a change that is the expression of a longer-term shift. In this case, adaptation is necessary.

2. This is in addition to all motivational effects. For example, if strong performers see that the company retains the poor performers with equal remuneration / opportunities, they may feel their contribution is not recognized and their efforts are not duly compensated, and they may either reduce their efforts or leave for greener pastures.

3. Or, better perhaps, he can congratulate them on being punctual the few times they do – thus reinforcing the good behavior.

4. The last scenario in the giraffes' example describes such a case.

3

THREE WAYS TO ADAPT

There are three ways in which individuals or populations adapt to their environment.[1]

Adaptation type	Affects	Manages tradeoffs which are	Involves natural selection?
Evolution	Populations	Stable	Yes
Calibration	Individuals	Volatile	No
Personal growth	Individuals	Volatile	Yes

Let's see them one by one.

Evolution

Groups of living beings adapt through evolution. Offspring are born with some mutations: random variations of their parents' genes. Those new genes can make the offspring more fit to the environment or less fit, depending on the specific mutation. Those whose genes make them less fit are less likely to survive and reproduce. The fitter ones, instead, get to survive and reproduce more. Therefore, on average, the fit genes get to reproduce more, and a higher percentage of the population of the next generation will have them.

This is equivalent to saying that **the average of the DNA of the population shifts towards the genes whose owners survived their environment.**

EVOLUTION

Manages stable tradeoffs in populations through natural selection

The unfit are harmed → the average DNA becomes that of the fit

The unfit are not harmed → the average DNA does not change*

(*): or drifts in a direction that does not increase survival chances.

Harm is the signal that directs evolution.

Evolution mostly manages *stable* tradeoffs *in populations*. This is because evolution can only take place when organisms reproduce, and once an individual organism is born, it cannot evolve. Therefore, evolution is well suited to adapt to slow, stable, long-term changes in the environment, which encompass many generations. Moreover, the beneficiaries of evolution are the offspring, the children of the fit who survived, not their parents. **Evolution adapts species, not individuals.**

However, in the face of volatile short-term tradeoffs, species also need some adaptive process to manage them to enable individuals to adapt to short-term shifts in the environment, like seasons or famines. Hence calibration.

Threat	Impact	Stability	Adapting process	Notes
A short famine	Light	Volatile	Calibration	
A long famine	Strong	Volatile	Evolution & Calibration	(*)
Decades of famine	Strong	Stable	Evolution	(**)

Notes:

(*) A famine lasting only a few weeks causes everyone to lose weight, including muscles (calibration). Instead, a famine lasting a few months causes everyone to lose muscles (calibration) and causes the weakest to die of hunger (evolution). Hence the presence of both adaptive processes. Therefore, not only the period (short-/long-term) must be analyzed to determine whether evolution, calibration, or both take place, but also the impact of the threat: did any individual die? If yes, then evolution is present.

*(**) Calibration is a byproduct of evolution, of course. **Evolution gives species the ability to calibrate.***

Calibration

Whereas groups of living beings adapt through evolution, individuals adapt through calibration. Some of their organs and tissues have the capability to increase or decrease their size or that of their cells. For example, humans are able to grow their muscles by going to the gym.

Calibration is a way to adapt to the subset of environmental volatility, which is likely to happen many times during an individual's life. For example, dogs can grow thicker fur during winter and lose it during summer. If they adapted to temperature using DNA changes alone, they would be stuck for their entire life with fur with constant thickness: a suboptimal solution, inadequate to both summer and winter. **Calibration allows individuals to adapt to their environment without having to change their DNA.**

Having a lot of muscles is usually a positive unless there is a famine, in which case it is useful *not* to have tens of pounds of muscles constantly burning energy. Being able to grow muscles only when needed and when resources are available ensures that we always have the optimal tradeoff between what is required and what we can energetically afford. Similarly, being able to grow and lose fur allows dogs to live comfortably during summers and to minimize energy warming themselves during winter. **Calibration manages volatile tradeoffs.**

Most of these tradeoffs are metabolic. For example, a person living a sedentary life does not need muscles and, therefore, loses them, allowing them to survive with less food: a useful adaptation in epochs when food was scarce.

Often, these tradeoffs are expressed via the following calibration rule: if there is a need for the organ/tissue to grow, then the organ/tissue is grown to fulfill the need; otherwise, it shrinks to gain metabolic advantages. For example, if sun protection is needed, the skin becomes tanned; otherwise, the skin remains fair.[2] Sometimes, the tradeoff can work in the other direction, especially if it is not metabolic: if there is a need to shrink the tissue, shrink it; otherwise, grow it. If a fur is causing overeating, lose it; otherwise, grow it. In general, the rule of calibration is that whether the organ/tissue grows or shrinks depends on the need for it. **Calibration optimizes tradeoffs by triggering tissue size changes *in response to need.***

How does our body know when there is a need for muscles, though? We do not grow muscle; we *regrow* it. When we go to the gym, if we lift a weight heavy enough, we tear some of our muscle fibers. Our body repairs them and/or grows new ones. If we do not harm our muscle fibers, we do not grow any muscle. **The need for growth is signaled by harm.** This concept is well explained in Nassim Nicholas Taleb's book *Antifragile.*

Moreover, when we tear some of our muscle fibers, our body regrows them *in excess.* This is necessary because today, we might have lifted 70 pounds, but tomorrow, we might need to lift 80. If our body only repaired the muscle fibers that got damaged, we would not be able to increase our muscle mass and, therefore, lift heavier objects if need be. In other words, muscles grow by overcompensation. **Harm triggers overcompensation.**

In some cases, calibration relies on indicators of future harm rather than on harm itself: *leading indicators,* which will be elaborated in later chapters. For example, some species of dogs use sunlight instead of the temperature of the environment to modulate their hair growth, relying on the fact that colder months are associated with shorter sunlight hours.

However, not all harm is good: only harm that can be survived is good for the entity receiving it. In a later chapter, we will explore the distinction between what constitutes "good harm" and what constitutes "bad harm".

In a nutshell, **moderate harm causes strengthening via overcompensation; the absence of moderate harm causes weakening.**

(In adaptive entities, of course. Non-adaptive entities, such as a building, are instead always weakened by harm: they do not have any over-compensative reaction.)

CALIBRATION

Manages volatile tradeoffs in individuals;
unrelated to natural selection

Harm → Overcompensation → Strengthening

Absence of harm → Weakening

Personal growth

Each person has a unique personality composed of patterns of feeling, thinking, and behaving. Let's call these *mental patterns*. For example, some mental patterns of mine are: I enjoy going to the gym, I like cheese, I default to "the other side is right" when I do not understand someone's behavior, I tend to nod a lot when listening to someone, I tend to fall asleep during boring meetings. Mental patterns might represent whatever association in someone's brain: what they feel, think, or do in a given situation or when facing a given cue.

A person undergoes personal growth when they adopt a new mental pattern that is advantageous (for example, the habit of regularly practicing physical activity or learning how to sustain an interesting conversation) or when they quit an old mental pattern that is detrimental (for example, the habit of spending too much time on social media or the habit of being late at meetings).

We constantly try new mental patterns or temporarily quit old ones, similar to how species try new genes by giving random mutations to their offspring. However, we adopt a new pattern for good only when it gets rewarded, and we quit an old pattern for good only when we acknowledge that it was damaging us. This is not too different from natural selection. In natural selection, the animals that are unfit for the environment get killed, whereas those who are fit get to reproduce. In humans, the mental patterns that are negative to us get us harmed, whereas those that are positive get us rewarded.

It is up to us to draw the link between the outcome (reward or harm) and the mental pattern that leads us to it (positive or negative). Associating a good mental pattern with rewards reinforces the habit; associating harm with a bad pattern that causes us to be harmed weakens the behavior, so that we will abandon it eventually. **If we fail to make the association, we risk letting the harm damage us without the negative mental pattern leading to the harm.** By preserving negative mental patterns, we put ourselves at risk of future harm.

If we were egoless, we would quit any mental pattern of ours that proves detrimental to us, and we would adopt any new pattern that proves to be beneficial. However, **we are not egoless, so we try to preserve our personality. By doing this, we hold back our capacity to adapt ourselves and to become fitter to our environment.**

Natural selection seems cruel: in the face of environmental changes, the unfit within a population die; as a consequence, the population adapts and becomes fitter. However, when it comes to humans, natural selection does not have to be cruel. Humans have a unique ability to adapt themselves; we call this "learning." An unfit person (someone who is poorly adapted to his environment) has the potential to adapt and become fit.[3] If he keeps being unfit, it is likely because he did not do what the fit did: learn.

If one refuses to let go of the traits of his personality that prevent him from being fit in his environment, then he will remain unfit,

and this will negatively impact his life: he will be left out of groups he could otherwise have benefited from, and he will not be able to secure opportunities which might otherwise have presented to him (he might get fired or not land his ideal job; he might be socially ostracized; he might not be able to find a good partner, and so on). If one does not adapt to his broadest environment, he will be at risk of being excluded from it.

PERSONAL GROWTH

Manages tradeoffs in individuals through natural selection

Ensuring that natural selection kills parts of us (negative mental patterns)
→ We adapt and therefore survive

Preventing natural selection from killing parts of us (negative mental patterns)
→ We do not adapt, and therefore we suffer

Chapter summary

There are three ways in which adaptation can take place:

- Evolution: the average DNA of the population shifts towards the genes whose owners survived their environment.

- Calibration: harm causes overcompensation; absence of harm causes weakening.

- Personal growth: by embracing evolutionary pressure and applying it to one's own mental patterns, an individual can grab the benefits of evolution, which are otherwise reserved for populations.

THREE WAYS TO ADAPT

EVOLUTION

The unfit are harmed → the average DNA becomes that of the fit

The unfit are not harmed → the average DNA does not change*

(*): or drifts in a direction which does not increase survival chances.

CALIBRATION

Harm → Overcompensation → Strengthening

Absence of harm → Weakening

PERSONAL GROWTH

Ensuring that natural selection kills parts of us (negative mental patterns)
→ We adapt and survive

Preventing natural selection from our negative mental patterns
→ We do not adapt and therefore suffer

1. Actually, there are more than three. For example, some octopods are able to change their DNA on the fly, some recent studies allege. However, only three adaptation processes are relevant for humans. Hopefully, no octopod is reading this book.

2. The tradeoff, in this case, is Vitamin D production. A skin that is too dark in an environment with not enough sun would not produce enough vitamin D. Conversely, a skin that is too fair in an environment with too much sun would get burned. Our skin, through calibration, adjusts the color of our skin to the optimal tradeoff of vitamin production – skin preservation.

3. Apart from a few exceptions, a healthy individual born in a first-world country has an incredible potential for personal growth.

4

ENSURING ADAPTATION

In the previous chapter, we saw that giraffes got taller if the trees they feed on got taller. The giraffe population reacted to harm – developing an adequate height was the reaction to the fact that those who did not grow longer necks died of hunger. Next, we will explore how **adaptation is a necessary reaction to harm.**

Imagine a group of giraffes living in a savanna with an absence of predators and an abundance of both short trees and tall ones. Also, imagine that suddenly, the tall trees grow even taller so that only a portion of the giraffe population can reach them, while the short trees remain short and accessible to all the giraffes. Assuming that there are enough short trees to feed all the giraffes, no giraffe will die because it could not reach the tall trees. Therefore, giraffes will not grow taller on average. **No harm to the unfit, no adaptation.**

Of course, there are a few other ways in which species can change – for example, genetic drifting. However, in this book, I only consider changes *that increase the fitness* to *the environment*. Forms of mutation that do involve a change that increases the fitness to the environment the population is exposed to are not considered an adaptation.

Adaptation at a population level takes place only if a change in the environment causes an imbalance in the survival or reproductive chances of the population. **If a change in the environment harms the portion of a population at one end of a spectrum, then the population will adapt towards the other end of the spectrum.**

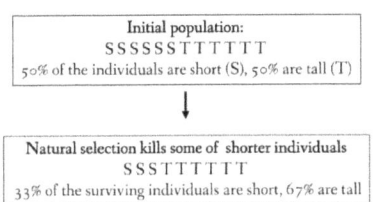

If the portion of a population at one end of a spectrum is harmed by a change in the environment, then the population will adapt towards the other end of the spectrum.

However, if the environment changes but the population is not harmed, then no adaptation takes place.

In a nutshell, **adaptation cannot take place without part of the population getting harmed.**

Adaptation to threats

Our environment contains a multitude of threats to our reproduction and survival. In the past, we faced a multitude of threats. For example, starvation by famine, death by a predator or a rival tribe, and being left childless because of our inability to procreate and/or protect our children from threats. In the present day and age, we face other threats: joblessness, homelessness, being socially outcasted, or being unable to find a partner.

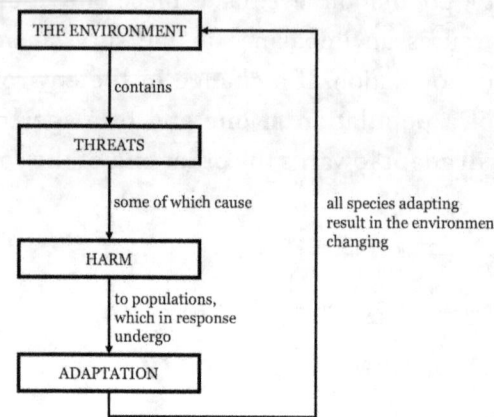

The environment contains multiple threats, some of which cause harm to populations, resulting in such harmed populations adapting to the threats and, therefore, to the environment.

The parallel adaptation of all species causes the environment to change, resulting in a cycle: the environment will be different, so some species will be more vulnerable to new threats, therefore getting harmed, thus adapting, and starting the cycle all over again.

We do not adapt to all threats

There exist three conditions which prevent a population from adapting to a threat:

1. The threat does not materialize.

2. The threat does not cause harm.

3. The population does not survive the harm caused by the threat.

Any of the three conditions is sufficient to prevent the population from adapting to the threat. As shown below, **adaptation happens only if *none* of the three conditions above take place.**

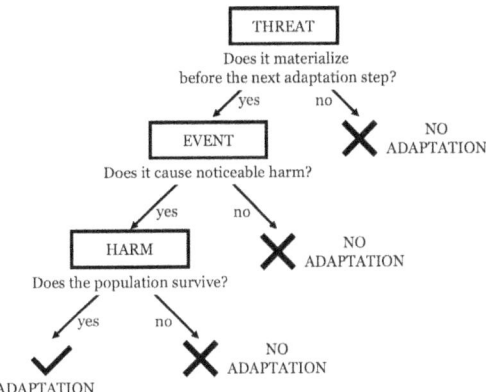

We already established that adaptation is always a necessity. Therefore, our goal is simple: to adapt as much as possible. And we do that by removing the three conditions that prevent adaptation. How to do that will be the topic of the next chapter.

Two questions

"Is it necessary to adapt to a threat that is not harming us?"

Yes: even if it has not been harmful to us yet, one day it might.

"But I have other priorities..."

Other priorities more important than survival or avoiding exclusion?

Being in synchrony with the environment

"Evolved" and "adapted" are both adjectives that express the same property: being in sync with the environment. **An individual or a population is adapted if they are not at risk of extinction from any environmental threats,** *regardless of whether they are perceived as threats at the moment.*

In general, civilizations that crumbled, organizations that disappeared, companies that went bankrupt, and individuals who died of non-natural causes were quite advanced and "evolved," possibly more than their peers; however, only towards what they *perceived* as threats, rather than to all threats.

Chapter summary

- Harm is necessary for adaptation.
- Any condition that prevents a threat from harming a population or that prevents the population from surviving harm also prevents the population from adapting.

In the next chapter

In the next chapter, we will examine the three conditions that can prevent a population from adapting to a threat.

5

THE THREE CONDITIONS THAT PREVENT ADAPTATION

In this chapter, let's examine the three conditions that prevent adaptation.

The first condition: the threat does not materialize

A volcano can stay dormant for centuries. A conflict can boil for decades. A financial crisis can take years to hit the markets. Sometimes, a threat does not materialize for years.

This can be a problem because **if a threat does not materialize at all for long enough, we adapt to its absence.** When a financial crisis does not take place for long enough, traders forget that crises can happen and take more risks, becoming more vulnerable to the crisis when it will inevitably happen.[1] When a driver does not make any incidents or does not lose control of his car for long enough, he will tend to drive more recklessly.

How long does the absence period of a threat has to be for living beings to adapt to its absence? Usually, the time it takes for adaptation to take place: an *adaptive cycle*. For animals and plants, it would be the time between generations (the time it takes for DNA to adapt;

in other words, the time for an individual to grow and bring offspring to the world, i.e., a new version of its DNA). For humans, an adaptive cycle means a much shorter period of time: the time it takes for one's feeling, thinking patterns and behaving patterns to get penalized or rewarded, and thus to be reinforced or abandoned. Humans are not only made of DNA but also of habits, beliefs, know-how, and automatic reactions. These are all mental patterns.

In general, for people, an adaptive cycle is the time it takes them to be judged, rewarded, or punished for their choices. For employees, this is typically the time it takes for them to get a bonus or a promotion (or to see their bonus or promotion going to someone else).

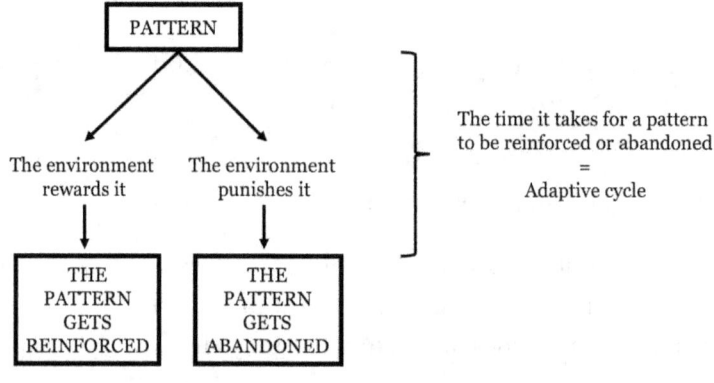

To understand this better, let's explore this using some examples.

Charlie is an ambitious first-year trader at an investment bank. Every year, the bank gives a bonus to traders whose investments produced enough returns. During his first year, Charlie made very conservative investments, which were very low risk but did not produce big returns. At the end of the year, contrary to his more risk-taking colleagues, he does not receive any bonus. Envious and frustrated, he decides to take more risks from now on. At the end of the second year, his investments produced larger returns, and his bank gave him a bonus. Euphoric about the reward and looking forward to more during the next period, Charlie starts his third year taking even bigger risks.

Let's examine the cycle: At the end of the first year, Charlie's conservative behavior did not get rewarded (no bonus is given), leading him to abandon the behavior in favor of a more risk-taking one, which paid off (bonus given) at the end of the second year. In this example, the adaptive cycle is one year: the time it takes for a behavior to get rewarded or punished.

This situation is dangerous from the bank's point of view. Judging the performance of its traders on a yearly timeframe causes it only to consider those risks that are likely to materialize within each year and to neglect those that are less frequent, even if they come with catastrophic consequences for the bank (consider that during a financial crisis, due to the extreme risks taken during the previous years, a bank is likely to lose more money than it realized in profits during all the years preceding the crisis). Humans tend to neglect risks that take longer than an adaptive cycle to materialize, dramatically underestimating their magnitude.

In other words, we humans are extremely good at both learning and unlearning. Unfortunately, this means that we are apt to unlearn what could be necessary for our survival if we do not happen to need it every year or so.

Biological adaptation takes place slowly but is also rolled back slowly. A species that took centuries to adapt to cold winters does not suddenly roll back its genetic mutations after a few warm years in a row. Instead, behavioral adaptation (such as the adoption of new mental patterns, a capacity unique to humans) takes place much faster but is also rolled back much faster. Take a village that learned for centuries to stock food to avoid starvation in case of a prolonged winter: it might take only a few warm winters in a row for some of its citizens to say that "long winters are no more such a thing" and that "excessive food reserves are unnecessary." If the town does not have systems to prevent such overadaptation (such as rituals, traditions, or respected elders reminding the young of the dormant threats), it can easily become vulnerable to threats that happen to be absent for a few years in a row.

The second condition: the threat materializes but does not cause harm

A threat that materializes but doesn't harm anyone is almost equivalent to a threat that doesn't materialize.

A few years ago, I met a man in his thirties who worked for a manufacturing company that used materials emitting cancerous gases. To my surprise, he told me he did not wear a breathing mask to protect himself from the vapors (he later told me, even though both the safety manager and his boss constantly reminded the employees to wear them). I inquired why he wasn't worried by the cancerous exhalation. His reply shocked me: "I've been doing this job for three years. If the gases were really that dangerous, I would have died already."

The man was clearly reckless. It is a possibility that cancer has already developed in his body, though it did not grow enough to be noticed yet. Moreover, exposition to most cancer risk factors is like playing Russian Roulette: the fact that you're still alive doesn't mean that it is safe; you might just have been lucky so far, and you better stop as soon as possible.

Some are wise enough to adapt to a threat that materialized but did not physically harm them – what is called a "near miss." However, for most people, a threat that does not harm them is a threat that doesn't exist. **If a threat does not harm them, they will adapt to the absence of the threat** as if the threat did not materialize at all. (Unless the near miss harmed them emotionally, in which case they would adapt at least partially to the threat.)

The reason people do not adapt to threats that do not harm them is that each adaptation comes with a tradeoff. An adaptation that has a benefit but makes the host vulnerable to a threat is disadvantageous in the presence of the threat but advantageous in its absence. If the threat is absent for long enough, such adaptation is likely to be picked up. When threats seem distant, we tend to choose adaptations that allow us to thrive over adaptations that allow us to survive.

For adaptation to take place, it is not only necessary that the threat harms people, but also that it noticeably harms them. For example, many people stop smoking cigarettes or eating sugary foods only when a doctor's diagnosis or some symptomatic illness make the harm visible, even though the sugar and the cigarettes have been harming them for decades.

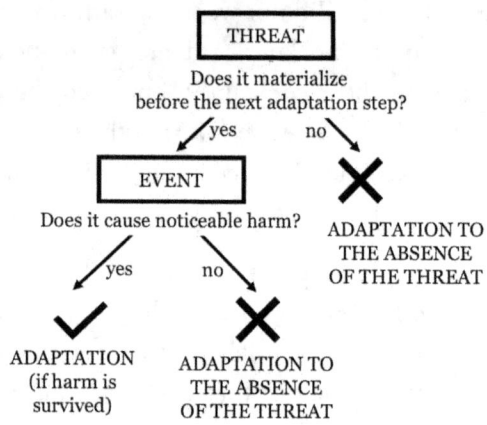

The third condition: the harm is lethal

If a plague kills the weakest 5% of the population, the rest will adapt to be more resistant to the plague. However, if the plague kills 100% of the population, then no one will be left to adapt. Some might consider the plague to be lethal if it killed some of the population. Though it was lethal for the people who died, it wasn't lethal *for the entity undergoing adaptation:* in this case, the population.

On an individual level, if an investor loses 20% of his funds in a bad trade, there still exists the possibility for him to learn and become a better investor; if, instead, he goes bankrupt, he will have no money to invest anymore (even if he is now, from a know-how point of view, a better investor).

Conversely, at the upper level, if 20% of a bank's traders make very bad trades and get fired, then the harm is lethal for the traders who got fired, but not for the bank, which got rid of its worst traders.

However, if the trades made by the bad traders caused the bank to go bankrupt, then the harm would be lethal for the bank as well, and there would be no adaptation for it.

Chapter summary

- Three conditions prevent us from adapting to a given threat:
- The threat does not materialize before we adapt.
- The threat materializes but does not harm us.
- The threat harms us, and we die before we can adapt.
- Any of the three conditions above is sufficient to prevent us from adapting.

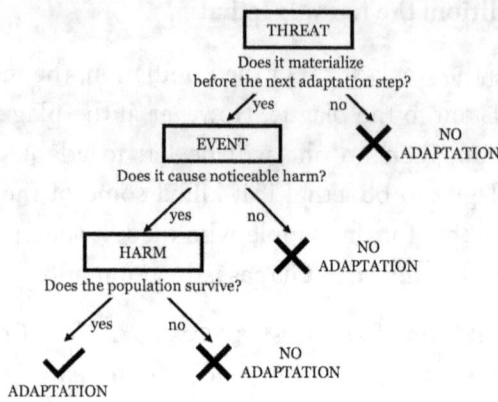

In the next chapter

In this chapter, I listed the three conditions that prevent adaptation.

In the next chapter, I will talk about what happens when the first condition takes place. Understanding how it works and the damage it causes is crucial for developing a strategy to avoid it.

---

1. Somehow, traders taking risks contribute to the genesis of the crisis.

6

OVERADAPTATION

L et's play a game. Imagine that I hold an opaque bag with an unknown number of colored tokens. For two hundred times, I put my hand inside the bag without looking, extract a random token, look at its color, *and then put it back in the bag.*

By doing that, I extracted 180 red tokens and 20 yellow tokens.

What do you think is the *percentage* of red tokens in the bag?

What do you think is the *percentage* of yellow tokens in the bag?

(Please take some time to answer the two questions above; only then, flip the page).

Did the sum of your guesses for the percentages of red and yellow tokens add up to 100%? What if I told you that in the bag there were also green tokens?

It turns out that in the bag, there were 80 red tokens, 19 yellow tokens, and one green token – which did not get extracted.

It would be a mistake to deny the existence of the green token simply because it didn't get extracted. Similarly, even if a storm of a given magnitude has never hit a given city, it doesn't mean that it never will.

When an event is rare and the observation period is comparably short, it might not be observed at all; however, that should not be interpreted as the event being impossible.

Blindness to the rare

Nassim Nicholas Taleb popularized Hume's problem of induction: people who never saw a black swan would think that all swans are white (even though, in Australia, swans are black). It is not because something has not been observed that it is impossible. However, we often forget this and conclude that what we did not see cannot be. It is our nature to use admissibility as a proxy for truth. More relevantly, **we tend to believe that what did not hurt us or any of our close ones cannot possibly harm us in the future.**

Adaptation exhibits similar behavior. Adaptation is a reaction to threats. If a threat does not manifest within one adaptation cycle, from the subjective point of view of the entity undergoing adaptation, it is as if the threat did not exist. Therefore, instead of adapting to the threat, it will adapt to the absence of the threat.

The more infrequent (compared to the length of the adaption cycle) a threat is, the more likely it is that adapting entities will adapt to the absence of this threat.

For example, if a financial crisis is less frequent than how long it takes for a trader to get promoted, then the trader will be incentivized to make decisions as if crises do not exist – unless, of course, the trader can be retroactively punished for taking risks; I examine this possibility in the next chapter.

A useful guideline is that threats that produce negative events of different magnitudes should be considered as separate threats, one for each magnitude.

For example, the river in my city floods:

- Every other year, 3 meters above its normal level (say).[1]

- Once every ten years, it is 4 meters above its normal level.

- Once every 30 years, it is 5 meters above its normal level.

Time period	Flood
Every 2 years	3 meters
Every 10 years	4 meters
Every 30 years	5 meters

Assuming punctual regularity, this means that over 30 years the following will take place:

Number of floods in 30 years	Flood height
15 floods	3 meters
3 floods	4 meters
1 flood	5 meters

Which yields an average flood of:
(15 x 3 + 3 x 4 + 1 x 5) / (15 + 3 + 1)
= 3.26 meters

THE AVERAGE
IS MEANINGLESS

Even worse:
if we consider
an observation period
of only 20 years,
the frequency table becomes

Number of floods in 30 years	Flood height
10 floods	3 meters
2 floods	4 meters

Which yields an average flood of:
(10 x 3 + 2 x 4) / (10 + 2)
= 3.17 meters

GIVING THE IMPRESSION
THAT THE FLOODS
ARE BECOMING LOWER

(whereas it's only the observation period which became shorter)

People considering those three different magnitudes of flood as a single threat would find it easier to talk about "the average flood." Therefore, they would be more likely to build a 4-meter wall by the river and say, "We adapted to floods, and we are not vulnerable to them anymore," even if they adapted to the 3- and 4-meter floods but are still vulnerable to the 5-meter one.

A better approach is to consider as separate threats the 3-meter flood, the 4-meter flood, the 5-meter flood, and the 6-meters flood (which is a threat: even if it hasn't materialized yet, it does not mean it will not happen in the future). Adopting this approach, it becomes more natural to say: "We adapted to the 3- and 4-meter floods, but we did not adapt to the 5-meter flow and the 6-meter one".

By considering threats that produce negative events of different magnitudes as separate threats (one for each magnitude), it becomes easier to spot those cases in which we lowered our vulnerability to the lower magnitudes only, and instead increased our vulnerability to the higher magnitudes.

Humans adapt fast

Most animals cannot adapt by changing their individual mental patterns; they only adapt through evolution. Therefore, they only adapt between generations, when one or two individuals produce offspring whose DNA is slightly different from that of their parents. Their adaptation cycle is quite long (years, for most large animals).

Humans are different. Humans are made of beliefs, habits, and knowledge – in other words, mental patterns.[2] You can think of humans as having a **"body DNA" made of genes** and a **"mind DNA" made of mental patterns**.[3] Humans can change their mental patterns in seconds. Usually, they change them when they are proven right (or wrong). Whenever a mental pattern gets proven right, it gets reinforced; whenever it is proven wrong, it is weakened or abandoned. Therefore, for humans, the **adaptation cycle for a given cate-**

gory of mental patterns coincides with the mean time to reward (or to punishment) related to that category. For example, the adaptation cycle of mental patterns related to work is the time between promotions or between bonuses awarding. For politicians, their adaptation cycle tends to coincide with the election cycle. For writers, their adaptation cycle is the time between books published. The common idea is that whenever a mental pattern gets rewarded or punished, it is reinforced or weakened (i.e., adaptation takes place).

In summary, due to our ability to adapt our mental patterns (our "mind DNA"), our rate of adaptation is faster than that of other living beings that do not possess this ability.

Adapting too fast

There are, however, instances in which this ability to adapt quickly works to our detriment – it can cause us to adapt *too fast*, therefore becoming vulnerable to those threats that lay dormant for a few years. I call this process *overadaptation*.

Therefore, it is important to be able to discern when overadaptation takes place in order to proactively try to reduce our vulnerability to the threats that did not take place recently. Two indicators of over-adaptation are:

1. The adaptation cycle is shorter than the mean time between negative events.

2. An individual after adaptation is very different than one before it.

If the first indicator is true but not the second, then even if an individual or population adapts to the absence of a threat, it will not adapt that much to be vulnerable to it when the threat materializes.

Overadaptation takes place when it is possible to adapt to the absence of a threat to the point of becoming vulnerable to it.

Predicting

Roman aqueducts built more than two millennia ago can still be seen standing in the European countryside, whereas a bridge built in modern times has a much shorter life expectancy. Why were the Romans so good at building aqueducts?

One hypothesis[4] is that Roman buildings are resistant because the Romans were bad at math (just think about how difficult it is to make multiplications and divisions with Roman numbers). If an architect is bad at math, he will find it difficult to precisely calculate how strong the building must be to withstand the environment; the evident solution is to build it so thick that it will stay in place for sure. Compare this approach with the modern one, where we use complex engineering models and software to optimize the thickness of the walls so that they are built with just enough materials to stand and to be cheap. **Modern architects optimized for efficiency; Roman ones optimized for durability. And both got what they wished for.**

(Wait! Aren't modern architects also wishing for durability? I don't think so, at least not unconsciously. Otherwise, they would produce stable buildings, not "stable buildings unless something unexpected happens." As I often say, **"Humans are extremely good at succeeding at their priorities and extremely dishonest about them."**)

The Romans' approach is not so different from that of animals and plants. As Nassim Taleb pointed out, **nature does not try nor needs to predict; it adapts.**[5] Similarly, the Romans did not try to predict. They realized that prediction might be imprecise, and thus built structures that could be durable regardless of assumptions about the future.

While trying to predict, we tend to make one common mistake: **when using the past to predict the future, we end up predicting the past,** which might not correspond to the future after all.

Risk homeostasis

In 1971, the Antilock Braking System (ABS) was installed for the first time as a standard on a new car model. The ABS is a device that prevents the wheels of a car from blocking when the driver brakes on a wet or slippery road. If you ever drove, suddenly braked, and felt the brake pedal pulsing under your foot, you know what the ABS is. How many lives do you think it saved from its beginning until the publication of this book (2018)?

None.[6] Or, better said, it saved a lot of lives but also caused many more deaths. While in theory, the ABS does increase the safety of drivers *provided they drive at the same speed as they used to drive before its introduction*, in practice, it encouraged drivers to drive faster, at the same *perceived* safety level.[7] In particular, the ABS reduced the number of non-fatal crashes (those where vehicles were going slowly) but actually *increased* the number of fatal ones[8] (most probably because drivers felt safe because of the ABS and now took the liberty of driving at higher speeds). Preventing the lightest incidents increased the perceived level of safety; the drivers responded by increasing their speed. Since high-speed incidents are much more likely to be fatal than low-speed ones, the ABS ultimately increased the overall number of deaths.

In general, **when allowed to choose between an adaptation that allows people to do something more safely or one that allows them to do something more efficiently or comfortably, humans tend to choose the latter. This is called risk homeostasis** and is a direct consequence of natural selection applied to mental patterns, a phenomenon which we will explore in the following example:

Imagine a driver in the late 70s, Dave, who has always driven along a given road at 40 miles per hour (mph, which corresponds to about 65 kilometers per hour). One day, Dave changes his car and gets one equipped with the ABS. It is safer, he is told[9]. In the beginning, he keeps driving at 40 mph. Many of the other cars that he encounters are driving faster. Dave feels bad because he could go faster, too. His conservative behavior gets punished and, therefore, weakened. One day, he decides to drive faster, at 50 mph. Nothing happens. He gets home faster. His risk-taking behavior gets rewarded and thus reinforced. Now, he drives home every day at 50mph. A couple of times, he had to make a couple of emergency brakings, but thanks to the ABS, his car stopped quickly, and no one got injured. Dave feels just as safe as he was when he was driving at 40 mph with his old car without the ABS. One day, unfortunately, Dave loses control of his car and goes off the road. No amount of braking can slow the impact. Dave smashes against a tree at 50 mph and dies. Had he been driving at 40 mph, he would probably have survived the impact.

Four considerations are important here.

First, Dave made **the mistake of conflating two threats into one:** incidents that can be prevented by braking and incidents that cannot be prevented by braking. The ABS only helped with the former, but he adjusted his behavior as if it helped with both – this is why it is important to consider similar threats as separate entities.

Second, Dave neglected that **while safety measures usually have a linear effect, negative events have a nonlinear impact.** Though the ABS might help reduce the distance necessary to slow down a car, the severity of an incident increases exponentially with the speed of impact. The ABS is great at preventing non-lethal impacts but less good at preventing lethal ones.

Third, **nonlethal negative events are usually more frequent than lethal ones. Being invulnerable to non-lethal events prevents the behavioral weakening that follows consequences after a non-lethal incident and, therefore, increases future risk-taking.**

Fourth, **risk homeostasis is the consequence of natural selection causing behavioral evolution.** We can imagine that Dave's mind is made of a population of driving behaviors: some behaviors are more conservative, and some are more risk-taking. Every time he drives home and no incident takes place, the risk-taking driving behaviors living inside his mind appear to be fitter than those that suggested more careful driving. As a result of natural selection, some of the most conservative driving behaviors (which appear comparatively less fit than the risk-taking ones) get excluded. The resulting average of the remaining population of driving behaviors is more risk-taking: the next time Dave drives, he will go slightly faster. Conversely, every time Dave drives home and an incident takes place in which he gets hurt (even just emotionally hurt or scared), some of his more risk-taking behaviors get excluded from the population of driving behaviors that lives inside his mind. The resulting average of the behaviors left will be more conservative, and the next time, he will drive slightly slower. Finally, if Dave drives home and he has a near miss, such as an emergency braking followed by no consequences, then his risk-taking behaviors will be unaffected. This further encourages him to continue his risk-taking driving behavior.

Chapter Summary

- If a threat does not materialize for long enough, we adapt to the absence of the threat.

- The more the time between adaptations is short compared to the time it takes for a threat to materialize, the more likely it is that we adapt to the absence of it (and therefore increase our risk-taking).

- The more we can change in a single adaptation cycle, the more we are vulnerable to threats that materialize infrequently.

In the next chapter

In the next chapter, we will review a few possible solutions to prevent overadaptation.

1. This is a hypothetical example. Please focus on the behavior of the population reacting to different "threat levels" rather than the absolute value of the numbers.

2. Some animals have mental patterns, too. For example, my friend's dog learned that he can get tasty snacks from his neighbor. However, the percentage of beliefs which are learned is negligible in respect to the percentage of beliefs that are innate in animals.

3. Obviously, I do not intend this literally.

4. The hypothesis comes from Nassim Taleb, *Antifragile,* page 223. Another hypothesis, probably complementary, is that roman aqueducts are still standing because the Romans knew how to enforce skin in the game: architects were required to stand under the bridge when the support used for building them was removed so that they would have some personal interest in making sure they were built properly (from Nassim Taleb's *Antifragile*, page 381).

5. Nassim Taleb, *Antifragile,* pages 68-69.

6. Source: US Department of Transportation. https://crashstats.nhtsa.dot.gov/Api/Public/ViewPublication/811182. See the following footnotes for details.

7. Unfortunately, people frequently use the frequency of incidents as a proxy for safety. They should instead consider the magnitude of their consequences.

8. Page 57 of the DoT report previously cited: "It demonstrates ABS is effective in preventing nonfatal-injury crashes (as opposed to fatal crashes)."

   Page 67: "On wet, snowy, or icy roads, every subgroup of fatal run-off-road crashes increased significantly for passenger cars. [...] Results were least consistent for collisions with pedestrians, bicyclists, and animals.

   The overall effect on fatal crashes was consistent between cars [...], but the observed effects on wet, snowy, or icy roads and non-fatal crashes (mostly collisions with animals) were not positive."

9. The ABS is safe only assuming that the driving behavior doesn't change (1st order safety). However, changes in behavior due to the presence of a safety device should be considered (2nd order effects). This phenomenon has been called "The Fence Paradox" by Pasquale Cirillo.

7

PREVENTING OVERADAPTATION

In the previous chapter, we saw how rewarding people faster than the expected frequency of negative events is a bad idea: if people adapt to positive events more frequently than they adapt to negative ones, they will adapt towards maximizing the number of positive events instead of adapting towards minimizing the impact of the negative events. In particular, we saw the example of an investment bank, where traders are given bonuses every year if their investments performed well but are never given any maluses even when they lose a lot of money, and how this is problematic as financial crises happen much less frequently than yearly. This entices the traders to engage in risk-taking behaviors and get rewarded with fat bonuses yearly (in the absence of financial crises); when the market crashes, though these traders receive no bonus, they receive no malus either. They profit from exposure to risks that others would pay (the bank and, in case of a bailout, society).

Both the problem presented in the paragraphs above and the solution presented in the next section appear in different variations across some of Nassim Taleb's books.

Skin in the game

Hammurabi's code, which ruled the Babylonians, contains the following lines:[1]

> *"If a builder builds a house and the house collapses and causes the death of the owner of the house— the builder shall be put to death. If it causes the death of the son of the owner of the house, a son of that builder shall be put to death. If it causes the death of a slave of the owner of the house— he shall give to the owner of the house a slave of equal value."*

By giving the builder "skin in the game," the Babylonians ensured that their houses were built stable.

Skin in the game requires that a person suggesting or committing an action that impacts a third party is also harmed in case the third party is harmed.

This concept can be applied to provide a solution to the problem we saw earlier for traders in a bank: to give traders a bonus when their investments produced profits *and* **a malus when their investments produced losses.** In addition, it is critical that those **bonuses and maluses are proportional to losses and non-dischargeable** (claw-back). If maluses were not proportional to losses, a trader would be comfortable taking huge risks that produce small yearly gains for many years and one huge loss concentrated in a single year: the result of the huge loss for him would simply be "no bonus this year," whereas for the bank it would be "endure losses much bigger than all the profits made during the past years."

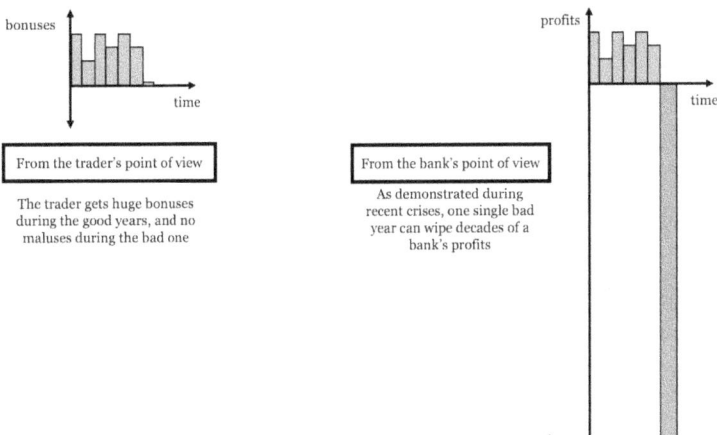

Maluses also have to be non-dischargeable. Otherwise, a trader could make risky trades that bring short-term benefits but also long-term losses and leave the bank after having cashed in the bonuses relative to the short-term profits but before having to pay the maluses relative to the long-term losses.

Though this solution addresses the issues from before, it has two practical limitations. First, it is easy to enforce proportional maluses but hard to enforce them over time, even after a trader has left the company or country in which he made the risky trades. Second, as per our human nature, we tend to overestimate short-term results and may, therefore, be incentivized to take risky trades nevertheless. To be clear, this solution is still very good and would bring great improvements were it to be implemented. By stating the limitations, I am in no way implying that it would be a bad policy; rather, I am its supporter.

In the next section, I will provide another solution that could address these shortcomings but has other limitations itself. I believe that the two solutions are complementary and would work very well together, each taking care of the shortcomings of the other.

The pyramid of risk

Herbert Heinrich noticed a relationship between incidents in factories. For each accident causing a serious injury, there would be about 29 accidents causing a minor injury and 300 accidents causing no injury. These exact coefficients were later disproved, but Heinrich was onto something: for each death, there are indeed many serious injuries; for each serious injury, there are many minor injuries; for each minor injury, there are several accidents causing no injury (also known as "near misses," for example, a brick falling from the roof but hitting no one), and for each accident causing no injury, there are many unsafe behaviors (such as a worker walking in the plant with no safety helmet). These relationships can be displayed as a pyramid, as in the image below.

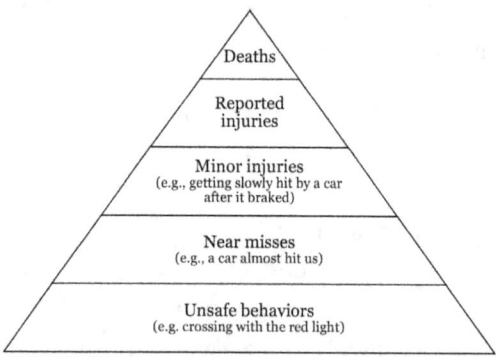

Now, let's do a thought experiment. Imagine that, in a fictional company, there has been one workplace death four years ago, one three years ago, one two years ago, and zero deaths last year. Can we say that the company became safer?

Time	4 years ago	3 years ago	2 years ago	Last year
Workplace deaths	1	1	1	0

No, we cannot. Perhaps the plant's current safety level warrants 0.75 deaths per year and last year, the employees of the company just got lucky. Maybe next year, there will be another death (or two). The sample is too small, and the results are too volatile. **Trends measured at the top of the pyramid are too volatile to have any predictive value.**

Now, let's imagine that in the same company, 25 employees recorded an injury four years ago, 30 three years ago, 15 two years ago, and 5 last year.

Can we say that the company got safer?

Perhaps; we cannot be certain. Though the sample is now large enough to enable us to spot more reliable trends, other possibilities might invalidate the results. It is possible that starting two years ago, the management covertly warned the employees and asked them not to report injuries. Also, there is the possibility that operations that produce light injuries did get safer but that the operations that cause no light injuries but might kill employees (such as electrical maintenance operations) did not get safer. Finally, trends measured in the top half of the pyramid lack data on improvements relative to rare threats. For example, employees may now have a lowered probability of injury from common sources of accidents but are perhaps still at a high risk of injury from infrequent ones, such as a fire.

Now, let's imagine that in the same company, random observations witnessed that four years ago, 50% of the employees were wearing a safety helmet in the areas where their use is required; three years ago, 80% of the employees; two years ago, 90% of the employees and last year, almost 100% of the employees.

Can we say that the company got safer? Yes, most probably. There is a correlation between the consistency of safe behaviors and how safe it is to work at a plant. Given that most incidents take place because of unsafe behaviors, the workers are safer now.

Trends measured at the basis of the pyramid of risk are more reliable, both because of a larger sample and because of a lower number of assumptions needed.

Moreover, indicators at the top of the pyramid have a disgraceful property: they measure events that already happened. For this reason, they are called *lagging* indicators. Companies and individuals that measure lagging indicators tend to be reactive: they only act when the lagging indicator is negative, i.e., after the negative event took place. Conversely, the indicators at the bottom of the pyramid can tell us whether negative events will occur *before* they happen. They are *leading* indicators. Companies and individuals that measure leading indicators tend to be proactive and usually manage to act to avoid negative events before they happen.

If a company only increases the frequency of safety trainings after a workplace death occurs, it is bound to have at least one workplace death. If, instead, a company increases the frequency of safety trainings the moment it notices that not all employees are following the safety guidelines, then it will probably be able to prevent the deaths.

Measuring trends at the bottom of the pyramid allows us to be proactive and avoid the negative event. Conversely, measuring trends at the top causes us to be reactive and to suffer from negative events.

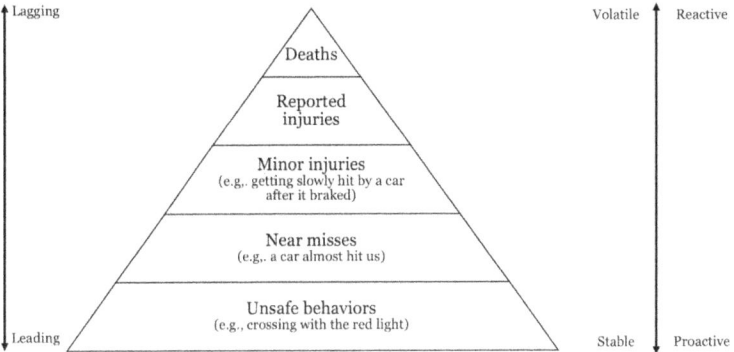

In the next section, we will explore how measuring trends at the bottom of the pyramid (in other words, considering leading indicators) can help to avoid overadaptation.

Using leading indicators

The second solution to the overoptimization problem would be to tie performance rewards to leading indicators rather than lagging ones, at least partially.

(I remind you that there are various types of performance recognition, including financial rewards, rewards of recognition and noticing the good, as well as disciplinary punishments or punishments in the form of admonishment. It doesn't only have to be promotions and bonuses or lack thereof.)

Overoptimization occurs when harmful negative events are less frequent than positive ones. **By tying consequences (rewards and punishments) to leading indicators rather than lagging indicators, the frequency of negative events increases, causing the incentive to optimize for the frequent small profits to disappear.** Let's explore this using an example.

A sales manager whose compensation is tied to his sales (a lagging indicator) will focus all his energy and time on making the numbers for the current quarter. If he has an additional hour, he will spend it on making one more phone call or on sending one more proposal. He will favor small, unprofitable clients who have a faster purchasing process over bigger ones, for which a sale might take quarters. He will try to squeeze every dime out of every deal, getting some short-term profits but damaging the long-term relationship with the client. He might even be tempted to sell defective products or products he knows would offer no benefit to that particular customer.

Conversely, a sales manager whose compensation is tied to leading indicators (such as client satisfaction, which is a predictor of repeated sales;[2] sales trainings attended, which are supposed to improve future sales; and customer research & qualification, which is supposed to improve the quality and profitability of customers) is more likely to bring great long-term results.

When I present the concept of the pyramid of risk and leading indicators, people tend to understand it rather easily. However, when putting it into practice, they often make a key mistake. They do pay attention to leading indicators, and they do measure them, but they fail to tie them to rewards and punishments. **If a bad performance on a lagging indicator does not impact the employee in any way, then he will not change his behavior.**

As illustrated in the chart below, only the top half of the pyramid is inherently linked to physical harm; consequences such as emotional or career rewards have to be actively tied to the indicators at the basis of the pyramid to ensure that employees change their behavior to improve them.

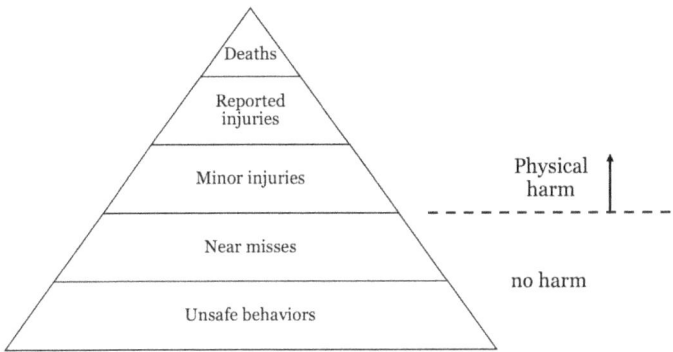

So far, we have focused on examples set in the context of organizations. In the second part of this book, *"Personal Growth,"* we will explore practical examples to show how to apply the principles described in this chapter to your own life.

Habits, systems and leading indicators

Bestselling author James Clear and cartoonist Scott Adams say that habits and systems (the day-to-day processes) are the keys to success, not objectives and goals. In the words of Hall-of-Fame American Football coach Bill Walsh, "The score will take care of itself" once the correct habits and systems are set. Habits and systems are leading indicators.

Measuring and improving leading indicators is equivalent to building strong habits and systems. They will lead you to create small daily improvements that will soon compound to important positive outcomes.

Happiness and leading indicators

Lagging indicators, those at the top of the pyramid, happen rarely. An objective can take years to achieve. Focusing only on them will cause you daily anxiety and dissatisfaction. Imagine you are working hard in order to get a promotion. Every day until the day you get your promotion, you will feel anxious, dissatisfied, or both. That's not a good life. Instead, the indicators at the base of the pyramid, the leading ones, happen daily. Focusing on them will cause you daily happiness. Every day, you will know that you are on your way to success because you are doing what it takes. That's a much better life.

Two complementary solutions

The two solutions presented in this chapter so far (ensuring skin in the game and the use of leading indicators) are complementary and, ideally, should both be applied. Skin in the game ensures that participants do not harm others, and the use of leading indicators provides them with a clearer path to succeed at their objectives.

Having to start with one, ensuring skin in the game is the way to go. It is the simplest of the two and requires less competence and oversight.

Case study: publishing 500 books

Isaac Asimov, the sci-fi writer most known for his "Foundation" series and the "Three Laws of Robotics," published more than 500 books in his lifetime. He achieved this with a simple system: sit down and start writing every day at the same time, no matter what. He clearly understood that books published are a lagging indicator, and writing is a leading indicator. Therefore, he focused on the latter.

Solving the sources of problems (rather than the problems themselves)

A subtle form of procrastination is to solve one's problems rather than to address their sources.

Each problem has a source. If you do not take care of it, it will generate problem after problem. **Solving a problem today without addressing its source means facing a similar problem again tomorrow.**

Paulo Coelho wrote: "When you keep encountering the same obstacle over and over again, it's life's way to teach you a lesson you don't want to learn." If you do not solve the source of your problems, new problems will keep appearing. (Another way to formulate the concept is: **"Problems grow the size they need to grow for you to acknowledge them"**).

A common prioritization tool is the Eisenhower matrix. It consists of a two-by-two matrix in which to classify items on one's to-do list *(see the figure below)*. The quadrants are: "urgent and important," "important but not urgent," "urgent but not important," and "not urgent nor important." The common interpretation of the Eisenhower matrix is to avoid working on the "not urgent nor important" items (which is correct), to delegate those "urgent but not important" (which is correct), and to work on the "urgent and important" while planning for later the "urgent but not important." This last piece of advice is one of the worst ones you'll ever encounter. The thing that most people do not realize is that **the very important is never urgent.** Planning the "very important but not urgent" means that the very important never gets done (because there will always be one more "urgent and important" thing to do). It's like saying, "We'll start closing the holes in the sinking ship once we get the water out."

The Eisenhower Matrix,
as commonly displayed

	Urgent	Not urgent
Important	DO	PLAN
Not important	DELEGATE	AVOID

In general, the very important is what addresses the root causes of problems that would surface in the long run and threaten us, and to build the fundaments for our long-term success.

Most problems appear to be "important and urgent," while the sources of those problems appear to be "important but not urgent." The trick here is to forget urgency and only work on the very important.

Some examples of the very important activities that people often chronically procrastinate include taking care of one's health, taking care of one's family, increasing one's skills and competencies, and working on one's habits.

Though there are consequences for not doing what is urgent, it is equally true that there are consequences for not doing what is really important (and apparently not urgent). Moreover, working on the sources of problems will reduce the number of urgent problems, whereas working on the urgent problems *will not* reduce the number of urgent problems – new ones are bound to be generated by the sources of problems that did not get addressed.

The person who feels stuck probably spent the last months only working on his problems and never on the sources of his problems.

Building on the concept we explored earlier of leading and lagging indicators, in general, **focusing on leading indicators tends to address the sources of our (present or future) problems, whereas focusing on lagging indicators tends only to solve problems temporarily and thus consolidate them as permanent.**

Furthermore, perhaps the most important point is that success is a lagging indicator, **whereas its causes, the leading indicators, are habits.** Bestselling author James Clear put it nicely: "**Your outcomes are a lagging measure of your habits.** Your net worth is a lagging measure of your financial habits. Your weight is a lagging measure of your eating habits. Your knowledge is a lagging measure of your learning habits. You get what you repeat."

Below are some examples of leading and lagging indicators.

Occupation	Example of leading indicator	Example of lagging indicator
Trader	Quality of decision making	Profits
Writer	Consistency and quality of writing	Works getting published
Person losing weight	*Consistency* of weight-losing habits	Weight lost
Student	*Intuitive* understanding of the topics studied	Grades / Academic success
Athlete/Freelancer	*Deliberate* practice	Success in his field

Case study: achieving results through the use of leading indicators

Before dedicating my career to independent research, I worked for three years with a manufacturing company that was renowned for its workplace safety and operational excellence. Some colleagues were hired to help another manufacturing company in Egypt to create a new production line on schedule. They focused solely on training the client's managers on workplace safety and on the behaviors of the managers (leading indicators). The result: the line was built on schedule. They understood that once the factors for success (the leading indicators) are in place, and a system for keeping them in place is present, then success follows naturally.

Success is a lagging indicator, and, as such, it follows leading indicators.

This case study also shows the importance of working on the sources of problems (lack of leadership and management skills) rather than on the problems themselves (achieving the project deadline).

Another use of leading indicators

Angela Jiang wrote: "The longer the time between action and result, the more room there is for charlatans." If the benefits of addressing the sources of your problems were immediate, it would be clear that this is what has to be done. However, working on the sources of your problems usually only shows benefits in the medium or longer term. This provides an opportunity window for charlatans to sell you "quick fixes" that might work in the short term but inevitably fail to produce any sustained result.

Leading indicators, by providing immediate feedback, help you focus your efforts on what is good for you in the long term.

Goodhart's law

Charles Goodhart pointed out that "when a measure becomes a target, it ceases to be a good measure." In other words, what gets measured (and rewarded) tends to get gamed. If too much importance is given to an indicator (be it leading or lagging), then people tend to adapt their actions to optimize for that indicator, even if it brings an overall negative result.

For example, tying bonuses and maluses to training attendance might lead employees to attend them without paying attention during training. Tying compensation to the amount of feedback given to the design team might lead salespeople to provide pointless feedback just for the sake of increasing the amount of feedback provided.

The key lies in choosing not only metrics that stand at the basis of the pyramid but also in choosing the least gameable metrics possible: metrics for which there is no possible way that they are increased with actions that are negative for the long-term success of the organization. Some examples:

- Giving a line manager a safety objective that is based not on the injuries registered but on the observance of procedures such as wearing helmets and gloves.

- Instead of giving a line manager a production goal, give them a quality one.

- Instead of focusing on your salary (which is somehow gameable by taking some position with a good starting salary but with little or no growth opportunities), focus on choosing a job in which you can learn a lot and which has great growth opportunities.

Traditions

Traditions and conservatism are, in a way, tools to prevent over-adaptation. By slowing down the rate of change in society, **the respect for traditions limits the enactment of policies that are dependent on volatile assumptions** or that have positive short-term first-order effects but negative long-term second-order ones, and in particular, those policies that might transfer risks from the individuals to the population.

Chapter summary

There are two complementary solutions to the overadaptation problem:

- Tying not only rewards but also punishments to indicators.
- Tying rewards and punishments not only to lagging indicators but mostly to leading ones.

Moreover, two very important concepts:

- Focus on addressing the sources of problems rather than alleviating the problems themselves.
- Success is a lagging indicator. Establish good habits (leading indicators) to pave your way to success (or your organization's).

In the next chapter

In the next chapter, I explore the second condition that can prevent proper adaptation: the absence of harm.

---

1. Nassim Taleb, *Antifragile*, pages 380-381.

2. A frequent comment is, "Client satisfaction is a function not only of the salesman but of the product as well. Salesmen shouldn't be penalized for a product that does not work." I argue that, instead, they should. What a wonderful incentive for salespeople to bring product feedback back to the design team!

8

THE HARM OF NO HARM

Nassim Taleb wrote:[1] "Small forest fires periodically cleanse the system of the most flammable material, so this does not have the opportunity to accumulate. Systematically preventing forest fires from taking place 'to be safe' makes the big one much worse."

When negative events do not materialize for long, and then they suddenly do, their consequences are often orders of magnitude larger than if they manifested sooner.

One reason is that the impact of negative events grows exponentially compared to the "inputs" or "catalyzers." A forest fire burning over two tons of flammable material is much more devastating than two fires distanced by some time, each burning over a single ton of flammable material. **Small negative events help to "clean the catalyzers."**

Small harm OR severe harm

Negative events happen. This is a fact.[2] We can delay them, but we cannot prevent them from happening forever.

We can often choose whether to delay addressing them until they are big enough to be unavoidable, at which point they will harm us significantly, or whether we will preventively harm ourselves so that we will withstand them with little trouble. Often, we are the ones who choose whether threats have the potential to devastate us; procrastination or lack thereof is the way we express our choice.

Mithridatization

Nassim Nicholas Taleb defines *mithridatization* as the result of **exposure to a small dose of a substance that, over time, makes one immune to additional, larger quantities of it.** In *Antifragile*, he tells the story of King Mithridates IV, whose father was killed by poisoning. Mithridates, not wanting to suffer the same fate, decided to regularly ingest small doses of poison, in a progressively growing amount, in order to build increasing immunity. By exposing himself to harm in non-lethal doses, Mithridates made himself more resistant to it. In other words, King Mithridates worked hard to force himself to adapt.

Similarly, in cases where we deem inevitable exposure to devastating events, we can protect ourselves from their consequences by preemptively exposing ourselves to less devastating versions of the same events.

We adapt to the absence of threats

If a threat does not harm the unfit, the unfit will get to reproduce as much as the fit,[3] and the population will adapt towards decreasing its chances of survival. Most adaptations represent trade-offs: some offer advantages to survival while providing other disadvantages, and others offer disadvantages to survival while providing other advantages.

For example, using one's full salary to live the high life without saving any of it offers an advantage (more social and entertainment opportunities), but it also offers a survival disadvantage (a vulnerability to bankruptcy in case of losing their job). If the survival disadvantage is temporarily negated (e.g., no layoffs for a few years), then the adaptation that provides the bigger non-survival-related advantage is the most likely to be selected for reproduction – decreasing the group's ability to survive when a threat hits again, for example when suddenly, layoffs become more common.

Harm does not have to be physical

Harm does not have to be physical to cause adaptation. Harm can manifest in multiple ways. For example, psychological harm (feeling bad after a rejection, feeling bad for not having gotten the promotion) **might be enough to trigger adaptation by weakening the unfit mental patterns and, therefore, making the individual fitter.**

Social harm that prevents one from mating at the same rate as a fitter individual is also another example of non-physical harm causing adaptation.

Optimizing for comfort brings discomfort

Too often, we organize our lives around maximizing comfort. I do not have any issue with comfort – it's great! – but I have an issue with minimizing discomfort.

Discomfort brings growth – up to a certain point, of course. I'm not advocating for living a spartan life full of discomfort. However, **a life with a pathological avoidance of discomfort is certain to make one weak and unfit to the environment (not to the environment he built around himself, a comfort bubble, but to the real environment, the one he will be exposed when, inevitably, the bubble pops).**

Not doing any physical activity is bound to make someone weak and prone to illnesses; similarly, avoiding any discomfort is bound to make someone weak and prone to harm. Just as spending every single instant awake at the gym is not the solution and will instead bring fatigue and injuries, neither is a good solution to throw oneself into too much discomfort.

The point is not minimizing comfort but avoiding minimizing discomfort.

In fact, **minimizing short-term discomfort is bound to maximize long-term discomfort.**

Discomfort will take place in everyone's life because the world is everchanging, and it requires everyone to adapt; it is everyone's choice whether to digest it drop-by-drop (and adapt) or to receive it all in a single, almost unrecoverable, blow.

Chapter summary

- Most threats accumulate when they are prevented from taking place, exponentially increasing their potential for harm.

- The absence of harm from threats leads to adaptation to the absence of threats, which increases the potential for harm.

In the next chapter

In this chapter, I write about the necessity of receiving harm in order to adapt. In the next chapter, I will warn against the opposite problem – receiving too much harm at once.

Then, I present some solutions to ensure that just the right amount of harm is experienced: enough to cause adaptation but not enough to cause too much pain.

1. *Antifragile,* page 101.

2. Unless we lived in an environment with no potential at all for negative events. This is clearly impossible: life is evolution; evolution requires natural selection, and natural selection requires negative events.

3. As I clarified in the first chapter, in this book, by "fit," I intend "apt to survive," not "apt to reproduce." Therefore, I am neglecting the effects of the ability to mate.

9

GOOD HARM AND BAD HARM

Harm allows us to adapt and learn. We learn that what caused us harm can harm us again and therefore, we have to make some changes to reduce our vulnerability to it in the future.

However, we need to survive the harm in order to learn from it. A dead student is hardly a good student.

Not all harm is good; only the harm that causes adaptation. Contrary to common thinking, not all harm is bad. The harm that triggers adaptation is good. A population needs harm to adapt; at the same time, it needs to maximize the chances that it can survive harm, avoiding extinction. Over the next two chapters, we will explore different types of harm and how to ensure that the harm we receive is a good one.

An adaptive entity, including you, your company, and our civilizations, should **have two priorities:**

- **Exposing its members to sources of good harm,** in order to suffer from just the amount of harm that will maximize positive long-term adaptation.

- **Adapting itself so that it will survive whatever harm it might have to suffer** (because of a miscalculating the risk it exposed itself to, or because of an unexpected event).

(Taleb's readers will recognize that the former is about voluntary exposure to negative non-tail risks, and the latter is about involuntary exposure to negative tail risks.)

It is to be noted that, while necessary, **proactive exposure to planned risks is not sufficient** to cover the first bullet point above; exposure to unplanned risks is necessary, too (otherwise, we end up vulnerable to everything that is outside of our list of risks to expose ourselves to).

A distinction

What causes muscle growth? Muscle damage. What causes muscle strain? Muscle damage.[1]

Where is the boundary between good damage (causing strengthening) and bad damage (causing weakening)?

The answer lies in damage distribution.

Damage distribution

The distinction between muscle damage that causes the muscle to grow stronger and muscle damage that causes strain is that the former is *distributed*.

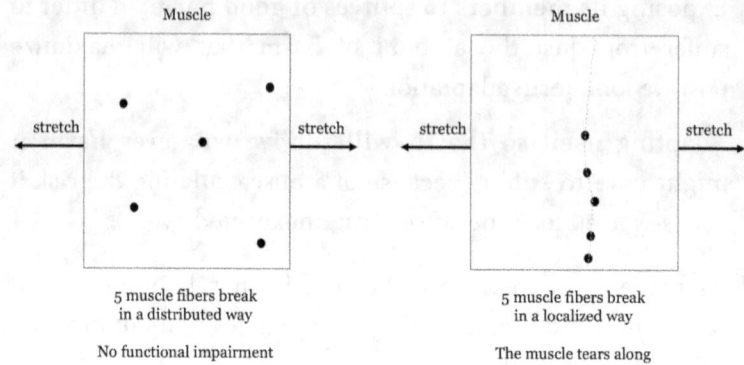

If lifting a weight, a few muscle fibers are torn in a distributed pattern, no muscle strain takes place. If, instead, too many fibers are torn in a concentrated area (a localized pattern), then a muscle strain takes place. The same happens with torn tendons.[2]

In general, **localized damage tends to cause functional disruption.**

Conversely, the damage that is sufficiently distributed does not only cause any negative long-term consequences; it actually produces positive adaptation.

If the damage is distributed, only the weakest die (the unfit). Conversely, if the damage is not sufficiently distributed, then there is a risk that even the fit die – if so, then no adaptation takes place.

Let's examine some other examples.

Adaptation and extinction are both the result of deaths.

Deaths of whom, though?

If no one dies, there is maladaptation: detrimental mutations are allowed to survive.[3] If the weakest members die, then the surviving population reproduces, and the population as a whole adapts. And if too many members of a population die, then the population becomes vulnerable to other threats – such as a tribe becoming vulnerable to a foreign invasion. In other words, **if the unfit survive, there is maladaptation; if the unfit die, there is adaptation; if the fit die, there is a risk for extinction.**

Moreover, in specialized populations, the distribution of deaths is also important. Did all the warriors die? If so, the population is vulnerable to invasion. Did most of the women die? If so, the population will have trouble managing the growth of the next generation. Did all the farmers die? If so, the population will be vulnerable to famine.

As another example, exposing one's mental patterns to being proven wrong is key to personal growth. However, exposing them all at the same time might cause all of them to be proven wrong at the same time – causing mental trauma that might prevent any learning. It is critical to ensure that only some of them can be hurt at the same time – in a distributed pattern.

Making harm good

Whether the harm is good or bad is not an intrinsic property of the source of harm but rather the result of the type of damage distribution that it inflicts on us. For example, lifting 100 pounds can cause good harm or bad harm, depending on the recipient. A weightlifter has muscles strong enough so that the act of lifting such heavy weights would only cause a few muscle fibers to be torn: good harm that would lead to muscle growth. An unfit person lifting the same weight would instead risk an injury: bad harm. In other words, **whether a given source of damage causes distributed or centralized harm is often influenced by the characteristics of the receiver.**

This means that there are three ways that we can use to maximize the chances that the damage we receive will cause distributed harm (and thus, good harm):

- Controlling the magnitude of the source of harm (for example, choosing the appropriate weight to lift at the gym).

- Becoming stronger (so that a given uncontrolled source of harm will inflict less harm on us).

- Using decentralization or "having more than needed" (both of which will be explained afterward) to minimize the chances that a given amount of damage distributes itself in a concentrated way.

Different damage distribution at different levels

Good harm is non-fatal: the receiver of the damage must survive it to benefit from it. However, it must be noted that **death at a given level does not imply death at the upper level**. A plague might be fatal for a person, who would perish without adapting, but not fatal for the population, which would benefit from the death of a few individuals dying and would adapt. "Fatal" always has to be tied to a subject. Damage that at a given level manifests as centralized (and thus bad) often manifests at the levels above as decentralized.

Similarly, a crisis resulting in a layoff is bad harm ("fatal") for the fired employees but good harm for the company (which gets rid of its lowest performers). A crisis resulting in a company going bankrupt would be bad harm for the company but might be good harm for the economy (which gets rid of its lowest-performing company). In this case, again, damage looking localized at smaller scales looks decentralized at larger scales.

Given a broad enough scope in both space and time, all harm is good (in other words, all harm is adaptation-producing). Though, of course, being humans, we would consider good only the harm that spares ourselves, our closest ones, our communities, and our species.[4]

Functional impairment

Good harm is non-impairing: if the receiver is left impaired, it becomes vulnerable to other threats.

Of course, a bit of common sense is necessary here. All harm is impairing. The difference lies in "slightly impairing" versus "very impairing". After a hard workout, a person is temporarily weaker. However, this fatigue only lasts a few hours and is not a big competitive disadvantage (the actual competitive disadvantage would come from not working out, which causes someone to be weaker and with less energy). Instead, a strained muscle takes much longer to heal and confers an important competitive disadvantage. In a fight, for example, the person with a strained muscle is unable to brawl effectively. The difference between the two conditions is the magnitude of the impairment and how long it will last.

Netflix & self-harm

In his *Incerto*, Nassim Nicholas Taleb describes how Netflix regularly applies "Failure Injection Testing,"[5] a program that purposefully creates failure scenarios for a restricted number of their users to see how the Netflix systems break and to adapt them so that larger outages do not take place. The key here is "for a restricted number": Netflix would be foolish to induce failure for all its users – imagine the bad press! However, Netflix understood that inducing failure for a restricted portion of them is exactly how to avoid failure for all of them.

Direct and indirect harm

The last distinction must be made between direct and indirect impairment.

The proper functioning of a population can be disrupted both by direct and indirect harm. Let me give you a few examples.

If a bridge collapses in my city, the traffic disruption will be caused not only by the fact that cars cannot use that bridge to cross the river (direct damage) but also by the fact that the cars which would have used that bridge will try to use other bridges, causing traffic jams there (indirect damage). Were the other bridges exceptionally fragile, they might even break under the increased traffic load.

Another example. Some ropes are made of twisted fibers. Let's assume that the fibers share the load equally.[6] Imagine a rope made of 100 twisted fibers, lifting a weight of 1000 pounds. Each fiber would have to sustain an individual load of 10 pounds (1000 pounds divided by 100 fibers). If the weakest of the 100 fibers breaks, only 99 fibers remain to sustain the weight of 1000 pounds. Now, each fiber must sustain a load of 10.1 pounds. The individual load increased by 0.1 pounds. This increase might cause another fiber – the weakest of the remaining – to break. Only 98 fibers would be left, each lifting 10.2 pounds. This increased individual load might cause other fibers to break, causing a chain reaction.

It turns out that while direct harm is a property of the individual vulnerability of each member of the population to the threat, indirect harm is also a function of the capacity of a damaged population to distribute additional workload.

In other words, **the more the members of the population are able to share loads between them, *even when some of them are unable to perform any work*, the less indirect harm the population will suffer** (for a given amount of direct harm).

The previous passage in italics is key. Most artifacts of the modern world are great at sharing work through specialized channels, *when they all work*. However, **what matters is not how well they work when things are all right but how well they work when problems arise** – especially those disrupting their internal functioning.

In *"Chapter 10 – Ensuring Survival,"* I will explain how to ensure that the condition above is satisfied.

Chapter summary

- Damage that is distributed enough has no negative long-term consequences and produces positive adaptation. Conversely, localized damage tends to cause functional disruption, which might or might not be fatal.

- Direct disruption is a function of how vulnerable each individual of the population is to threats; indirect disruption is also a function of the capacity of a damaged population to distribute additional workload.

- Good damage (damage that produces adaptation) is damage that causes distributed harm without being fatal or causing any disruption that would make the population vulnerable to other threats. Whether a given source of damage causes distributed or centralized harm can often be influenced by the choices of the receiver.

In the next chapter

In this chapter, we have explored the distinction between good harm and bad harm. Next, we will explore how to benefit from the power of adaptation through exposure to good harm.

---

1. And, of course, what causes muscle reduction? Absence of harm (and of nutrients).

2. Not only spatial distribution has to be considered when assessing whether the damage is localized or distributed, but temporal distribution has to be considered as well, in some contexts. For example, a continuing series of hits without time for recovery might break a tendon.

3. If no one dies, doesn't it mean that they were all fit? Shouldn't it be good?

    Not necessarily, for two reasons. First, they might just have been lucky: perhaps, during their lifetime, winters were extraordinarily warm, or their neighbors decided to wage wars elsewhere – exceptional conditions unguaranteed to repeat themselves.

Second, perhaps they did survive because they were fit. However, the fact that no one died in the present generation necessarily means that the following generation will be less fit (unless they properly implemented a lifestyle that included the practices described in this book and managed to adapt from harm without having to suffer death).

4. To be more correct, in this context, "our species" = "whoever we consider human."

5. http://techblog.netflix.com/2014/10/fit-failure-injection-testing.html

6. From an engineering point of view, this is not fully correct. For the sake of the example, let's assume it is.

10

ENSURING SURVIVAL

Nassim Nicholas Taleb makes the following example.[1] In Russian Roulette, the player grabs a 6-barrel gun loaded with a single bullet in a random position, takes it to his head, and presses the trigger. One out of 6 times, he dies. Five out of 6 times, he survives and collects a prize, let's say 1 million dollars. On average, a Russian Roulette player will win 83.33% of the time (five out of six times); his expected payoff seems to be $833,333 (83.33% times the payoff, $1,000,000). However, if the Russian Roulette player repeats the game a few times, his payoff will not be $833,333 multiplied by the number of times he will have pressed the trigger, but $0. Eventually, the trigger will hit the bullet in the barrel and kill him.

In repeated games where a "game over" is possible, the notion of an expected payoff is meaningless.

Those games are especially vulnerable to the survivorship bias. We only hear from those who survived them and benefited from them.

(As I say, 5 out of 6 economists think that the Russian Roulette is a safe game, and the rest couldn't be reached for comment.)

Avoiding the game over

I call "game over" the moment when an individual is expelled from a population without the possibility of returning to it.[2] It might be death (an individual abandons the living), but also personal bankruptcy (an entrepreneur/investor leaves the population of entrepreneurs/investors), corporate bankruptcy (a company leaves the population of companies in an industry), being fired (an employee leaves the company), being exiled (an individual leaves the population of a country) and so on.

Whenever game over is possible, the concept of average expected return ceases to make sense. "Average" requires a large number of iterations (for the law of large numbers to kick in), but the game over prevents an individual from surviving long enough to achieve this large number of iterations.

Consequently, it does not make sense *for us individually*[3] to expose ourselves to any risk that might cause us to experience game over. Sure, there are cases when we might want to expose ourselves to risks that cause game-over: namely, if *not* exposing ourselves would also cause game-over. For example, for an inmate facing death, it might make sense to expose himself to fatal risks while attempting to escape from his prison. However, **the statistical expectation of a net gain alone is never a sufficient reason for exposing ourselves to the risk of game-over.**

The way to go is generally to expose yourself to risk while making sure that game over is not a possibility. Over the rest of this chapter, I will discuss how to do that. One last point to clarify before that.

Having more than needed

The first way to mitigate the risk of game-over is "having more than it is needed," in particular, **"having more than it is needed** *according to the present assumptions" – since such assumptions might change, and since even though such assumptions have a confidence interval, events might still happen outside that confidence interval.*

In other words, **instead of trying to be *righter*, try to be less vulnerable in case you're wrong.**

There are different ways to achieve redundancy; here are the most common:

- **Keep resources uninvested.** First, it means not betting more than you can lose. Second, it means never betting with borrowed money, aka leverage (for a detailed explanation of how leverage works, please read this footnote[4]). Third, it means not betting everything but keeping resources on the side because you might need them at some point. (By betting, I do not only mean "playing with money," but also "investing"; moreover, I do not intend only "betting money," but also other kinds of resources, namely time: do not take too many commitments, because a sudden additional commitment you can't refuse might cause you to fail at the other ones.) Keeping resources uninvested has, of course, opportunity costs. I do not suggest keeping *all* your resources uninvested. However, you should consider keeping *enough* of them uninvested. **The goal of efficiency should never take precedence over the goal of survival.** By the way, being the one who has resources to spare when things go bad is a competitive advantage.

- **Be stronger than needed.** Buildings should be thicker than needed because the next flood, storm, or earthquake might be stronger than the strongest that ever was. Similarly, you should bring more value to your job than is needed, be physically stronger than is needed, and so on.

- **Reduce assumptions or assume uncertainty.** The more assumptions are made, the more things can go wrong. The less you make, the fewer things can go wrong. Assume uncertainty.

The behavioral impact of having more than needed

Without redundancy, you will not be able to adapt. **Adaptation requires harm but also survival.**[5] Adaptation requires the unfit to die but also the fit to survive.

Having no redundancy does not only prevent you from learning from your mistakes, because a single mistake can wipe you out, but it also prevents you from risking making mistakes, causing you to live in a limbo where you do not try anything that might result in a mistake, and therefore end up not adapting, unfit, and vulnerable. For example, a person whose family depends on him hanging on his job is much less likely to take any career risk.

A person with redundancy can take more (non-potentially-lethal) risks and, therefore, increase his chances of incurring adaptation. A person who has a healthy bank account and competencies relevant to the job market can afford to take career risks and has, therefore, more opportunities to test new approaches and, therefore, learn and adapt.

The downside of having more than needed

On the other side, **having more than needed prevents us from feeling harm and, therefore, adapting.** For example, living in a very unclean space is clearly bad for our health, for we are at risk of infections. However, living in a space that is too clean is also bad for us – preventing any exposure to germs leads to a weakening of our immune system.

Clearly, the former condition is much worse than the latter; I am warning about the risks of the latter because they are very underestimated, and **underestimating risks can make them become consequential.**

As another example, a speeding fine causes most drivers who receive it to adopt safer driving habits. However, a $50 speeding fine for a millionaire (who has "much more money than needed") is unlikely to hurt him and would, therefore, not influence his habits, putting him at a higher risk of injury from reckless driving.

The car manufacturer Toyota is famous for having successfully implemented a concept called Lean Manufacturing[6]. Lean Manufacturing considers a warehouse a waste because it requires workers to move components from the suppliers' trucks to the warehouse and then again from the warehouse to the manufacturing plant; moreover, a warehouse costs a lot of money to build and operate. Much better to have the suppliers deliver the components "just-in-time" so that the workers only have to move them once from the truck to the plant.

Not Lean: trucks → warehouse → plant

Lean: trucks → plant

Saving the costs of operating the warehouse and moving the components twice is only one of the benefits of lean manufacturing, though. The second is that **the absence of buffers causes problems to surface and become urgent, incentivizing their resolution, thus ultimately improving the system.** Buffers aren't only bad because they represent unnecessary costs but also because they shield the system from the symptoms of structural problems. Continuing the previous example, if a warehouse is present and the supplier's truck is one day late, it is no big deal: the workers just use the components already stocked in the warehouse without noticing the structural problem (an unreliable supplier). Conversely, if there is no warehouse, the first time a supplier's truck is late, production is delayed. You can bet that the problem will be solved as soon as possible, and a possible source of risk for the system will be removed. Obviously, it would not look for shocks that had the potential to put the whole company in trouble. Toyota understood that adaptation requires looking for harm, but only distributed and non-lethal one.

Leading indicators: the solution to a dilemma

Now, we face a dilemma: if we are not as strong as needed, then one risks game over, but if we are much stronger than needed, then adaptation does not take place because we do not suffer any harm. Both being too strong and not strong enough prevent adaptation. **The solution to this dilemma is, again, attaching consequences to leading indicators.**

Some examples:

- Have a stacked warehouse in order to be able to continue operations the day the supplier's truck is late (having more inventory than needed), but work immediately with the supplier to ensure that the next time he will not be late (in this case, a truck being late is the leading indicator, whereas the warehouse running out of parts would be the lagging one).

- Make clear to your employees that they have some freedom to operate (shielding them from career risk) but give them frequent feedback on what they are doing correctly or incorrectly (leading indicator) so that you do not find yourself in a tight spot when things go really bad (lagging indicator).

- Make sure that you set aside some time each week to learn new skills (to have more skills than currently needed) but make sure that you spend it on learning skills that will be useful by putting them to use as soon as possible to see how they work (leading indicator) and to practice them (another leading indicator), or by ensuring that the skills are relevant to your market *and* that you're progressing on them (again, leading indicators), to avoid spending too much time learning ineffectively or learning something ineffective (lagging indicators).

Referring to the previous examples:

Situation	Recommended situation	Leading indicator	Lagging indicator
Stacked warehouse	More inventory than needed	Supply trucks being late	Warehouse running out of items
Give your employees some freedom to operate	More job safety than needed	Frequent checks	Final outcome of their actions
Learn something new regarding your craft each week	More skills than needed	Frequently try to practice what you learnt to see how it works	Your future competency and success

Direct and indirect game over

There are two ways that risks can negatively affect us: by threatening our survival, or by threatening the survival of the population we are a part of.

In general, things can go well for us for two reasons: they go well for us individually, or they go well for the group of people we are part of (and we indirectly benefit from it). Similarly, things can go bad for us for two reasons: they go bad for us singularly, or they go bad for the whole group of people we are part of (and we indirectly get afflicted). For example, an employee can lose his job because he was doing a poor job (and got individually fired), or because his company didn't manage to turn in enough profits and had to close the business, thereby firing him and his colleagues (regardless of their individual contribution).

Of course, fixing one's individual contribution should be the priority. The few people who got this covered should also focus on their group's, because if their group does not adapt, they might indirectly suffer, too.

Chapter summary

- In repeated situations where a "game over" is possible, the notion of an expected payoff is meaningless.

- Having more than needed helps in preventing game-overs.

- Having way more than needed also prevents adaptation by nullifying the harm of smaller negative events; attaching consequences to leading indicators offsets this and keeps adaptation vibrant.

Further readings

Nassim Nicholas Taleb's *Antifragile* and my book *Ergodicity*.

In the next chapter

In the next chapter, we will examine new metrics that can correctly evaluate future fitness to the environment, in order for us to know whether we are correctly adapting to our environment.

1. Nassim Taleb, "Skin in the Game: Hidden Asymmetries in Daily Life" (2018).

2. Some authors refer to the risk of game-over in this context as the "risk of ruin."

3. As seen before, exposing ourselves to game-over does not make sense for us individually, but it does make sense for the upper layer: it does not make sense for a trader to expose himself to bankruptcy, but it does make sense for the population of traders to have traders exposing themselves to bankruptcy, so that the worse traders are expelled out.

4. Leverage means using borrowed money to invest. For example, I can buy a share worth $100 with 2x leverage. Simplifying, it means that if the stock goes up by $1, I get $2, but if it goes down 1$, I lose $2.

    Continuing the example, if the share I bought at $100 goes down to $80 before going up to $150, and I invested with a 2x leverage, then I make $100 ($50 x 2). However, leveraging is dangerous. If I invested with leverage 5x when the stock was down 20$, I would be down five times that, $100: the value of my investment would be $0, and my bank would kick me out of it, leaving me with no money and no chance to benefit from the following raise in price. Leverage is dangerous because it limits how much a stock in an *average* upward motion can *temporarily* go down before the investor loses his investment and, therefore, loses the chance to benefit from a following increase in price.

    The more volatility there is, the more dangerous leveraging is. Actually, once we consider 2nd order effects, we notice that **leveraging is always dangerous**: the less the volatility, the more investors are tempted to leverage, and the more they become at risk if volatility suddenly rises (for a practical example, just google what happened in early 2018 to those who invested in VIX).

5. Again, it is critical to clarify which layer is the subject of adaptation. Adaptation of the individual requires the survival of the individual; adaptation of species requires both the death of the unfit individual and the survival of the species. Layers should not be confused.

6. Business schools often incompletely describe Lean Manufacturing as "waste reduction"; a better definition would be "adaptation catalyzer".

11

THE NECESSITY OF BOTTOM-UP

Problems are often tackled with a top-down approach. The problem is analyzed, a few solutions are mentally formulated, and the one that seems the most admissible is selected and then put into practice. The top-down approach seems logical and makes a lot of sense. However, it often doesn't work, or seems to work until suddenly it doesn't.

The bottom-up approach

A more practical and effective way to proceed is the bottom-up approach. No assumption is made about the problem, which is solved through trial and error. A first solution is tried, possibly on a small scale, without too many expectations of it working. If it works, great! Even if it does not make any sense. If it doesn't work, it is immediately abandoned, even if it makes sense. Then, the bottom-up practitioner tinkers a bit with it and tries again and again, until suddenly, it works.

The necessity for bottom-up

Top-down solutions are very attractive: they seem to make sense. However, that is exactly the problem. They seem to make sense because **top-down solutions got selected because they easily made sense and not because they work.**

It is foolish only to check whether first-order effects make sense. The wise, instead, check whether first- *and* second-order effects *work* without caring whether they make sense.

(First-order effects are those that take place before populations and the environment adapt to them, whereas second-order effects are those that take place *because* populations and the environment adapted to the first-order effects. For example, raising tax rates generally has a first-order effect of increasing tax revenue and a second-order effect of increasing tax evasion and elusion. In the previously cited example of the ABS, the first-order effect was to reduce the number of car incidents, and the second-order effect was to increase its severity because drivers adapted to the apparent safety by increasing their driving speed.)

There is an abundance of top-down solutions and a lack of lasting results from them. We need more bottom-up solutions. The goal of this book is to get you to implement bottom-up personal growth. Its results might be slower but will last forever. What is achieved the bottom-up way is stable.

Why is the bottom-up stable?

The bottom-up is stable and long-termed because it derives from adaptation and has already been subject to natural selection. Thinkers go through many iterations and expose their prototypes to many "natural selection" events; they drop what does not work and improve what works; as a result, their inventions tend to be more resistant to the test of time. Conversely, academics dump ideas without submitting them to the test of practice and without exposing them to harm. As a result, they are necessarily less stable and less resistant to the test of time and to the real world.

What is born out of the real world resists it; what is born in a bubble bursts as soon as the bubble itself is exposed to the real world and bursts.

Characteristic	The top-down way	The bottom-up way
Approach	Theoretical	Practical
It is based on	Wishes	Experience
Criteria for choice of solution	Does it make sense?	Does it work?
The practitioner considers the ultimate judge to be	Its peers	Reality
Has it already been subject to natural selection?	No	Yes
Therefore, does it work in the long term?	No	Yes

The top-down is unstable because it is reliant on assumptions and, therefore, crumbles when they change. Instead, the bottom-up is stable because it does not rely on any assumption.

Some examples

Here are some examples of comparisons between the top-down and the bottom-up:

- Top-down happiness is short-lived (such as "I will do X, or buy X so that I will be happy"); bottom-up happiness is long-term (such as being happy thanks to your closest ones). The former is top-down because it originates from a theoretical idea of what should be done to achieve happiness; the latter is bottom-up because it lets experience define what makes you happy without deciding it yourself.

- Top-down passion is a mirage (choosing a job because it matches a preexisting passion seldomly works); bottom-up passion lasts (becoming passionate at a job you're doing because you're getting good at it). This is because the former is an expression of what we wish reality was but do not really know because we have not experienced it yet, whereas the latter is an expression of experience.

- Top-down success is short-lived (such as people who get picked for TV programs because of connections), whereas bottom-up success is long-lived (such as people who become actors or singers because they're good at it).

- Top-down theories tend to get disproven (theories where the researcher starts with an idea about how things should be), and bottom-up theories tend to get proven (theories where the researcher studies an idea without wishing for any theory to be true). This is because bottom-up theories are an expression of what is happening, whereas top-down theories are an expression of what sounds admissible to happen.

- Top-down innovation is rarely innovative (the results of academic innovation are mostly incremental, if any at all). In contrast, bottom-up innovation is innovative and produces life-changing results (tinkerers are usually those who produce the innovations that actually improve our quality of life). This is because top-down innovation is mostly concerned with doing what feels admissible and with justifying what the inexplicable happens, whereas bottom-up innovation does not care about whether it is admissible or why it works, only whether it does.

- Top-down relationships fail (relationships in which partners are chosen based on whether they fulfill a checklist of wished attributes), whereas bottom-up relationships tend to succeed more frequently. This is because the former still have to endure a reality check, whereas the latter are born out of it.

- Top-down peace is unstable; bottom-up peace is stable. (When a nation or group of nations tries to achieve peace with some military intervention in a land that is not theirs, or by drawing borders on land that is not theirs, what ensues is usually war or dictatorship, not peace. Just look at the 20th and 21st-century history in the Middle East: most initiatives whose intention was to stabilize the region actually made it more unstable, once second-order effects kicked in.) This is because top-down interventions assume a static world and forget to account for how local populations and individuals will adapt to the interventions.

The problem with top-down adaptation

Natural selection only works when the environment decides who gets excluded from it; otherwise, adaptation takes place with respect to a non-representative sample of the environment. It follows that no one can arbitrarily decide what is unfit and has to be replaced – the environment has to be the judge.

In the first chapter, I wrote that no adaptation could take place without the unfit dying or being harmed. I immediately clarified that "the unfit dying" does not mean, neither should be, the death of the unfit *individuals*: the desirable path is, instead, the removal of the unfit mental patterns *from* the individuals, to be achieved through bottom-up, self-directed personal growth. In this way, both individual, organizational, and societal adaptation are achieved without unnecessarily harming any individual or depriving them of their own free will and right of sovereignty over their body and mind.

However, I fear that a few people might read the first part of this book only focusing on the necessity of adaptation and then propose or advocate for top-down solutions to the adaptation problem. For example, some might claim that some form of ethnic cleansing (killing the unfit) could be good because it would make the population progress. No. Not only would it be an atrocity, and not only could such a system be abused in many ways; also, deciding who or what to kill or to harm is an arbitrary top-down act and, therefore, bound to bring negative long-term results. **For results to be long-term, the environment has to be the sole judge.**

Similarly, people might suggest performing the "personal growth" process in a top-down way, deciding which mental patterns people should try to cancel from their personality. Again, this is wrong. Not only for obvious ethical reasons but because, again, it would be a top-down act. Top-down adaptation is always wrong and always detrimental in the long term. One cannot decide what is bad for another; they might let that individual find out by exposing himself to the environment and letting it decide.

Learning

Some might ask whether reinforcing a mental pattern through learning is a bottom-up or a top-down endeavor.

Reading is a good way to learn, but only when one uses reading to critically collect inputs to be later applied in practice to judge their validity. Reading is a bad way to learn when one tries to directly encode the patterns written in the book to their own mind without first letting them through some kind of filter *based on real-world experience.*

For example:

- Reading a guide on how to write a book will do little good alone. Instead, a more effective process is to actually start to write a book, applying 1-2 suggestions from the guide, seeking feedback, validating whether the applied suggestions were effective, and repeating the process over and over in incremental iterations.

- Reading a book on famous investors alone might do little good to your investing abilities and might even be detrimental in case of survivorship bias: you do not know if the author of that book, who is telling you to repeat what he did to become rich, got rich because of what he did or despite what he did. Is he teaching you how to become rich, or is he like a lottery winner telling you how to pick the lucky numbers? Only filtering what he has to say through your filter of personal experience (trying what he proposes), of vicarious experience (did other people who did the same things *in another period of time*[1] end up with the same result?), and of common sense (would what he is saying make sense to your grandma?).

The pattern here is that **reading provides top-down solutions; however, by putting in practice selectively critically-filtered pieces of such solutions and exposing them to adaptation, you can make them bottom-up.**

Chapter summary

- Top-down solutions tend to be short-lived; bottom-up solutions work long-term instead.

- Bottom-up solutions work because they've already been through natural selection and, therefore, already adapted to the environment.

Further readings

Taleb's *Antifragile* also covers the topic of the bottom-up.

More examples of the importance of the bottom-up in decision-making can be found in my essay *"Optimizing for the wrong metric,"* available at https://www.luca-dellanna.com/optimizing-for-the-wrong-metric

The QR code to the article mentioned above

In the next chapter

Now that we have explored and understood the benefits of a bottom-up approach over a top-down one, in the next chapters, we will explore how we can harness the power of bottom-up adaptation in our personal lives.

1. Otherwise, they might just have gotten lucky for the same reason as the author. Like saying that "choosing 56 as the lottery number" is good advice because other people won the lottery with that number *on the same day*. In this case, the temporal coincidence means that what looked like many instances of success are actually a single one. Restricting the environmental input to a single period of time means introducing the assumption that the future will be like the past, which is quite unlikely.

PART II

PERSONAL GROWTH

A 4-step system

Let's embark on a 4-step system that will help you leverage the power of adaptation to achieve personal growth.

Each of the four following chapters represents one of the steps.

12

THE FIRST STEP: RECOGNIZING THE NEED FOR CHANGE

"Life doesn't care about your problems. The day you get over this is the day you'll grow. People want the world to change but don't want to change themselves. This is narcissism, pure and simple. You feel as though your problems deserve to be treated differently, that your problems have some unique math to them that doesn't obey the laws of the physical universe."

— *MARK MANSON*

The first step for personal growth is to acknowledge the need for change and for personal growth, after which, in later sections, we will explore how to implement change and further growth.

Let go or be let go

As we saw in the first part of this book, given that the world is constantly changing and adapting, one of the following two scenarios is bound to happen. **Either you let go of those parts of you that are inadequate for the world you are living in, or the world will let go of you.**

"But I should not have to let go parts of myself"

It is understandable that you want to hang on every single bit of who you are right now. Like everyone, you don't want to be happy; you want to be happy on your terms.

You are entitled to decide your terms for being happy. You are not entitled to the world accepting them.

It doesn't mean that you should change all of yourself. Everyone has a unique personality. However, it does mean that you should change some parts of yourself – in particular, those that are preventing you from fulfilling your potential (however you define it). You are entitled to be yourself – and others are entitled to decide whether to engage with you. Probably, you want to be able to distinguish between the mental patterns that make part of yourself (and keep them, being confident that you will find people who enjoy them) and those mental patterns that instead are limiting you from reaching your potential (and changing them). For example, being an introvert isn't necessarily something you should change; however, being able to present your ideas in public is definitely a skill you want to acquire.

The terms of your work

Similarly, it doesn't mean that you have to work the job that society wants you to work or that you have to work the best-remunerated job. Instead, it means that whatever job you might decide to pursue, you will not be able to decide all its terms. There might be parts of your job in which you can, and should, innovate and be inflexible about, and others in which instead you should do what the environment (the market) needs. **Being able to differentiate between the two is a key skill.**

Adaptation is bottom up

We have already seen that **evolution is bottom-up.** Species do not decide how they want to evolve – they create random mutations, and then the environment decides what works. **Successful individuals and organizations do not decide *how to* adapt – they decide *to* adapt and then let adaptation happen.** They do decide what to try, but they do not decide whether to stick with it. I am not saying that an individual or organization cannot succeed by only executing top-down decisions; I am saying that when they do, it is either by luck rather than by any reproducible process or because they tried tens of different top-down approaches, failed at most of them, and eventually found one that the market appreciated (of course, trying many top-down approaches and letting the market decide which work is actually a bottom-up process).

Sometimes, successful companies do something that looks like top-down but is actually bottom-up: a relentless focus on leading indicators. Because they headed where no one else was heading, they appeared as top-down visionaries; often, they were only followers just like everyone else; simply, they decided to follow leading indicators rather than lagging ones. Using a contemporary example, part of Amazon's success came from its refusal to optimize for earnings (a lagging indicator) and from its determination to focus on building a strong offering and strong sales and delivery channels. As another example, Steve Jobs decided to focus on extraordinary design; however, his products were the results of multiple iterations. By the way, Steve Jobs did not follow a top-down vocation in becoming one of the most famous product designers; his youth consisted of cluelessly trying different things (and seeing what works, which is a bottom-up approach).

If an individual or an organization decides *how to* adapt rather than just *to* adapt, it will risk adapting in ways and directions that do not improve its chances of survival. To be clear: we need to initiate adaptation in a certain direction; the key point is to acknowledge that our first step is just a tentative one, a way to gather evidence to decide then where to take the next step, and so on. What is to be avoided is to take the first step with the intention of taking the next hundred in the same direction and stubbornly decide not to change direction even when evidence is telling us that it would be better to do so.

It is the difference between deciding to go out to eat at our favorite pizzeria, finding it closed, thinking that today it might be its closing day, and changing our mind to go to another restaurant we might like, compared to ruining our night by spending it sitting in front of it, in the cold, waiting for it to open.

Similarly, it can be challenging if you want to decide not only the next step in your career but your career as a whole. If you do, you will be in for a lifetime of frustration. You can decide to grow, and you can decide what to try – but you can't decide the results. The environment determines the results- what works and what does not. **If you already knew *how* you would grow, you would have grown already, wouldn't you?** The fact that you still have to grow means that there is something you do not know yet, and if you do not know it yet, you can't decide what it is that you do not know yet. (People who think that they know what they do not know are the worst learners.)

Likewise, you cannot decide whether a relationship will work. You can decide to try a new relationship, and you definitely shouldn't try it if you didn't expect that it *could* work, but you shouldn't expect that it *will* work, and you shouldn't try *too* hard to make it work. You can do whatever is in your circle of competence to make it work, but you shouldn't try to step outside of it. If the two of you aren't meant for each other, it will not work. Any attempt to deny this will lead to unhappiness, either by delaying the inevitable breakup or by preventing it but leading to a relationship full of sadness and resentment.

Evidence that something doesn't work shouldn't be treated as a sign to try it *harder* but as a sign to try it *differently* or to try *something different*.

Happiness is bottom-up

Similarly, **you cannot decide *how* you will be happy.**

Consider the subtle difference between the two sentences below:

- You just need to decide to be happy in order to become happy.
- You just need to decide *how* to be happy in order to become unhappy.

The former describes embracing the bottom-up; the latter describes embracing the top-down. (The first sentence does not intend a behavior of passive acceptance of whatever comes, but the proactive search for happiness through working hard to improve one's self, but without deciding beforehand how one will be happy, but by trying many things and accepting the one that makes us happier.)

If you have anecdotes of people who decided how to become happy and then became happy, you will notice that their happiness was short-lived. For example, people who decided to marry in the hope that it would fill their lives, or people who decided to spend their savings buying a lot of material stuff not because they need it but because they think that it would make them happy.

Consider two people, Alice and Adele, both working a boring office job and both deciding to quit it to dedicate themselves full-time to painting, with the hope that they would become happier. Alice never seriously tried painting, but she thought she would enjoy it – because who wouldn't want to spend her days doing something creative? Adele instead had been painting in her free time for a few years and already knew she was rather good at it and liked it. Who do you think will be the happiest after a couple of years? The chances are that Adele, who adopted a bottom-up approach, will be quite happy, whereas Alice, who adopted a top-down approach, will still feel the same void and boringness she felt during her office job.

> *People want to be happy on their own terms,*
> *and therefore end up unhappy.*

Be humble

Be open, and avoid assuming in advance what is good for you.

Becoming an adolescent is about discovering what is good for others; becoming an adult is about discovering what is good for you.

We can say that the first stage of our life is about listening to what others tell us to learn about the world; the second stage is about ignoring what others tell us in order to learn about individuals; the third stage is about ignoring what we are telling ourselves in order to learn about ourselves.

For a healthy person in a first-world country, the problem is seldom getting what she needs but rather knowing what it is that she needs.

Do not think as your present self

It is perfectly understandable that you do not want to change a part of yourself.

However, understand that if you do change, it will not be your past self to judge who you became – but your future self. Your present self might not like your future self – but your future self might love it. Don't be shy about changing.

Don't be lazy

Letting the environment decide how you will grow does not mean that you should let the world do all the work. Conversely, it means: **do the work, and let the world decide the results for you.** If you do your work properly, the results will be good.

Many of the most appreciated people in their field did not follow a linear career path – they often shifted focus on their life in a seemingly random way until success struck – but they also did not wait for success to happen – they understood they had to put in the work.

The fact that most of your work will not be acknowledged does not mean that you would have been able to do what you will be acknowledged for without it. Most probably, it was vital for you to build competencies and connections and to understand what works for you and for the market (the environment).

Don't be emotionally lazy

Being happy requires doing your work *and* growing up. **Growing up is mostly emotional work – being able to observe yourself, your mental patterns, the results of your mental patterns, acknowledging that some of your mental patterns are detrimental, and letting them go.** Too many people only do physical work – spending all their energy on doing, and not a single bit on changing themselves, and then being frustrated because their situation isn't changing. Forgetting that their situation is a lagging indicator of themselves.

"But I don't want to change"

You don't have to.

In this book, I'm not telling you what you should do. Only you have the right to decide that. I'm only telling you how to start the process of personal change in case you would want to, what will happen if you do it properly (happiness), and what will happen if you do not do it (unhappiness). But, of course, you have the right to be unhappy.

Do I have to adapt to everything?

No, only to leading indicators.

Adapting to lagging indicators will cause you to adapt to the past, preventing you from growing. Adapting to leading indicators will enable you to adapt in preparation for the future, enabling you to grow. (More precisely, adapting to lagging indicators causes you to adapt to present results, which are children of the past; adapting to leading indicators causes you to adapt to present results, which are predictors of the future).

For example, if you are a photographer, do not try to maximize the number of likes your pictures generate (a lagging indicator) – focus on improving your skills (a leading indicator); the likes will follow.

If you are a graduate looking for your first job, do not try to maximize your salary (a lagging indicator); focus instead on landing a job with good growth opportunities and where you can learn a lot (both are leading indicators). The salary will follow.

Further readings

The appendix essay "Ego and Decision Making" delves deeper into the concept of not thinking as your present self.

13

THE SECOND STEP: HOST A MULTITUDE

In Chapter 3, we saw that for personal growth to happen, we must let the environment apply the threat of harm to our mental patterns so that the least fit ones get abandoned, fitter ones get created or reinforced, and we adapt as a result.

There are **two prerequisites** for this:

- To perceive yourself as containing a **fluid multitude of mental patterns (thinking patterns, behaving patterns, feeling patterns)**

- To perceive those **mental patterns not as *parts* of yourself but as tools *for* yourself.**

The former point is indispensable in allowing you to perceive feedback not as directed toward yourself but toward one of your mental patterns. The latter is indispensable to allow yourself to let go of the mental patterns that reveal themselves ineffective.

Andrew Ruiz makes the following analogy: on a laptop or a phone, we do not have a single app; we have a multitude, and we use the one that suits the most our current goal at any time. Similarly, we can be a multitude of patterns, use the best ones, and let go of the worst ones, all of this without identifying with any of them.

In Chapter 10, we saw that to ensure that the harm we receive is distributed – and therefore good – it is helpful to be "decentralized." Considering yourself as having a multitude of mental patterns is a good way to "decentralize" yourself and ensure that you can safely remove the faulty ones without endangering the ensemble – you.

Being vs. not being a multitude

SCENARIO: Mark is an office worker. Mark has not been promoted for years. One day, his boss tells him that his presentations are boring.

- NOT BEING A MULTITUDE: Mark processes this feedback as "my boss thinks I am boring" and therefore does not try to learn any presentation skills, or if he does, he does not *actually* try to apply them.

- BEING A MULTITUDE: when his boss tells him that he is boring, Mark understands that the boss is not addressing him, but his presentation skills (a mental pattern of his). Moreover, Mark understands that his boss is not addressing all of his presentation skills (his chart-making skills are excellent) but his monotone voice (another mental pattern of his). So, Mark takes a course to improve his speaking skills. Mark also knows that he is not his own voice, and therefore feels no obstacle to practicing new manners of speaking or to adapting his current manner of speaking to the situation – similarly to how some people have no problems, or even enjoy, choosing the most appropriate dress for the event at hand.

SCENARIO: Jim always wanted to write sci-fi novels. He submitted a few, but none got accepted for publication. One day, he gets offered a job as a copywriter.

- NOT BEING A MULTITUDE: Jim refuses the job offer: his dream is to publish a sci-fi novel. To get by, he must get a job as a waiter. Fast-forward twenty years, and Jim is still a waiter and still has not published any novel.

- BEING A MULTITUDE: Jim accepts the offer to work as a copywriter. He understands that writing sci-fi novels is only *one* of his passions and that perhaps he might get interested in other fields as well. By spending the first few months doing deliberate practice while copywriting for his clients, he quickly improves his skills. His clients now pay him well and trust him; because of that, he starts to love his job. Fast-forward twenty years, and Jim is a renowned copywriter. He feels accomplished. Moreover, his writing skills improved. Last year, he took some time off to write a sci-fi novel. It got accepted and will be published soon.

Granular change

Being a multitude is the necessary condition for being able to change granularly.

If you perceive yourself as containing a multitude of patterns, you will have no problem receiving feedback not as personal but towards one of your patterns – and you will, therefore, be able to change the mental pattern without losing your sense of identity. If, conversely, you do *not* perceive yourself as a multitude of patterns, you will perceive all feedback as personal, and therefore, you will be unable to change your mental patterns – you will see them as inseparable parts of yourself.

Proposed Exercises

- Think about a friend or colleague of yours whose presence you enjoy. What are some mental patterns of theirs that you like? Can you find a mental pattern of theirs that has a negative impact on their life?

- Think about a person you dislike. Can you list the mental patterns of his or hers that you dislike? Can you find a mental pattern of theirs that you like or at least find positive?

- Think about the last few pieces of positive feedback you received. Do not consider them as related to you but to one or more mental patterns of yours. To which mental pattern(s) were they directed? Can you find a way to express them more often?

- Think about the last few pieces of negative feedback you received. Do not consider them as related to you but to one or more mental patterns of yours. To which mental pattern(s) were they directed?

Chapter summary

- **Host a multitude:** consider yourself an ensemble of mental patterns, none of which are representative of yourself.

- **Hosting a multitude prevents you from taking feedback personally and enables you to use feedback to improve your mental patterns.**

14

THE THIRD STEP: EXPOSE YOURSELF

The door sign said: "Everything you need to be a hero." Many opened it, but backed away when they saw no equipment, only horrible situations.

— O. WESTIN

The third step is to increase your exposure to the environment and to practice your craft so that you can see which mental patterns of yours work and which do not, after which you can test new ones to see if they work.

Deliberate practice

The old saying goes, "Practice makes experts." However, not all kinds of practice do. Some people seem to have been practicing their field for years, yet they have not shown any improvement after achieving basic competence. Others seem able to proceed towards mastery steadily. What differentiates the former from the latter?

The former engages in **a form of practice that is closer to busywork: he repeats the same movements over and over again, does not get feedback (or, if he does, he ignores it), and generally desires that his work would be different so that he could succeed in it. The latter, instead, engages in deliberate practice: he tries new mental or action patterns, looks for feedback, defends the feedback rather than himself, is quick to internalize it, and generally desires to improve so that he can succeed at his craft.**

Busywork practitioner	Deliberate practitioner
Looks for his comfort zone	Looks to exit his comfort zone
Repeats the same patterns	Tries new patterns
Avoids feedback	Looks for feedback
Defends himself from feedback	Defends feedback & internalizes it
Perceives pain as negative	Perceives pain as positive
Wishes he could remain the same	Wishes he could change faster

To engage in deliberate practice:

- You should **proactively try to exit from your comfort zone.**

- You can do so **by adopting new patterns:** action patterns (how you do what you do), thinking patterns (the assumptions behind why you do what you do and why you do it the way you do it), and feeling patterns (how what you do makes you feel and how you react to it). Bestselling author Stephen Covey says that there is a space between an event and our response. We often cannot prevent or influence events, but we can *always* decide how to react to them, provided we survive them. For example, I might not be able to prevent a traffic jam, but I might decide to be okay with it because it will give me more time to listen to an audiobook or to think about how to organize my next days.

- You should **proactively look for feedback** to maximize your learning opportunities. Make sure you ask for it from people who will not sugarcoat it.

- Once the feedback arrives, you should not defend yourself but **defend the feedback**, defaulting to "the feedback is right; what mental pattern of mine generated that feedback?" [1]

The main characteristic of deliberate practice is that it is proactive. The deliberate practitioner knows where he wants to get and does everything he can to get there – not outside of the practice, but inside the practice. The deliberate practitioner does not look for shortcuts – he knows that practice *is* the shortcut. The deliberate practitioner looks for (controlled) pain: he knows that it is the indicator of growth. The deliberate practitioner internalized the previous point: effort does not bring him pain anymore, but pleasure – the pleasure of improving his own condition.

Practice is the shortcut

Too often, we look for shortcuts to avoid doing the hard work that leads to success (however we might individually define it), whereas **practice is the actual shortcut to success** (or, at least, long-term success). All other "quick fixes" that promise us "instantaneous results" are detours we take from the path to positive outcomes.

Avoiding the game over

As discussed in chapters 9 & 10, take calculated risks, ensuring that their negative consequences can never be fatal.

Take small risks to make yourself less vulnerable to unforecastable risks.

Tinkering

The biggest inventors of all time were all tinkerers. Tinkerers do not spend too much time thinking about how they can succeed; they try new approaches, see what works, see what doesn't, and change accordingly. Then, they try again.

The Wright brothers, the inventors of the airplane, were not the only ones trying to figure out flight. Another company, with more people and a larger budget, competed with them. And yet, the Wright brothers ended up inventing the airplane. How? The other company was testing a new prototype about once per month; the Wright brothers, once per day. The Wright Brothers were tinkerers.

Similarly, you can be a tinkerer with your own mental patterns. Expose themselves to the world's feedback – see what works and change what doesn't. Then repeat.

Good feedback and bad feedback

So far, in this part of the book, I wrote that some feedback is to be accepted and used to decide which mental patterns of yours to change. However, not all feedback is to be accepted.

Only follow feedback from leading indicators, not feedback from lagging indicators.

Feedback from leading indicators will make you grow. Follow all feedback that indicates that you are learning, that your skills are progressing, and so on.

Feedback from lagging indicators will do nothing for your growth. Lagging indicators are predictors of past performance, not of future one. If you follow the feedback from lagging indicators, you will be fit for the world that was, not necessarily for the world that will be. Feedback from lagging indicators includes salary, social media likes, page views, and so on.

If you have to choose a job, choose learning opportunities and future career opportunities over salary (provided it can sustain you, of course) – the latter alone does not do any good in predicting your future growth.

Moreover, **everyone follows lagging indicators. Following lagging indicators will bring you where the competition is, making it harder to thrive. Instead, following leading indicators will bring you where competition isn't (yet), making it easier to thrive.**

Proposed exercises

1. Think about an area of your life you would like to improve in (a sport, a hobby, a skill, a work task, a relationship, etc.)

2. Schedule an opportunity to practice it. Do the scheduling right now.

3. Choose a specific sub-result for your practice session. If you chose to improve your basketball skills, for example, it could be "try to always stay within one foot of the player you're defending"; if you chose to upgrade your cooking, it could be "cook the meal just enough so that it's crispy outside"; if you chose a work task, it could be "automate it so that you could do it in half the time." What matters is that you choose something that is both specific and measurable.

4. Keep changing the way you are doing what you are doing until the result is reached. Do not focus on the pain and frustration but on the satisfaction of improvement instead. Do not focus on doing more or faster; focus on doing differently. During the whole practice, think: which mental patterns should you acquire? Which should you lose because they are impairing you?

Chapter summary

Engage in deliberate practice:

- Proactively try to exit from your comfort zone.
- Proactively try to adopt new patterns: action patterns (how you do what you do), thinking patterns (the assumptions behind why things are happening the way they are happening and about what they mean), feeling patterns (how things you encounter and things you do make you react to them).
- Proactively look for feedback.
- Once the feedback arrives, defend the feedback rather than yourself.

---

1. However, do not accept all feedback – only that which comes from leading indicators. This is explained in this chapter's section called "Good and bad feedback."

15

THE FOURTH STEP: LET GO

The fourth step is to let go of those mental patterns of yours that proved ineffective. As Ben Thompson said: "**admitting when you're wrong is the fastest and shortest way to being right.**"

As seen earlier in the book, if there is no harm, there is no adaptation. And unless the unfit is let go, there is no adaptation. If you try to preserve your mental patterns from being harmed, then you will not be able to grow. You need to let go of your ineffective patterns in order for yourself to become more effective.

Always direct feedback to your mental patterns, never to yourself

You should never take feedback personally, but always take it as directed to one of your mental patterns. The problem is never you; it is always one of your mental patterns.

Similarly, when one of your activities gets boring or unpleasant, try to relate the negative feeling not to the activity itself but to one specific aspect or instance of the activity. For example:

- Do not tell yourself that you do not like your job – perhaps you do not like *that aspect* of your job.

- Do not tell yourself that you do not like running – perhaps you do not like running *in the cold*.

- Do not tell yourself that you do not like learning – perhaps you do not like learning *from that medium*.

Some mental patterns hold you back

One of my favorite quotes of all time is:[1] "Getting your sh*t together requires a level of honesty you can't even imagine. There's nothing easy about realizing you're the one that's been holding you back this whole time." I would add **that it is important to realize that it is not you who has been holding you back but some of your metal patterns.** Acknowledging this last point will make it easier to accept the insight above.

Other mental patterns propel you forward

Similarly, when you succeed at something, it is easy to attribute your success to yourself. A more effective approach is to attribute it to a mental pattern of yours (and acknowledge that part of your success was due to luck as well). **By linking your success to a pattern of yours, you will be able to reinforce that pattern** and ensure that you practice it more often, yielding further success.

Other authors, such as Chip & Dan Heath, suggest a similar technique called "Bright Spot Analysis." It involves analyzing your days or projects, drilling down on the most productive ones, and asking yourself, "What did you do that time that was different and led to effectiveness?". Of course, **the goal of the technique is to find out which condition or mental pattern was the cause of the success** and then *figure out a system to ensure that you are in that condition or are using that mental pattern as consistently as possible.*

Revisiting mental patterns

What got you here won't get you there, wrote Marshall Goldsmith. Some mental patterns are beneficial only during some phase of your life and are harmful afterward. The behaviors that will get you hired for your first job are different from the behaviors that will lead to your first promotion, which in turn are different from the behaviors required to get promoted as a manager.

Being able to entertain the possibility that something that worked well for you in the past might be the same thing that is holding you back now is a key life skill.

Let go of the mental patterns which are unfit

If a leading indicator makes you understand that a pattern of yours will prevent you from achieving what you could achieve, then let go of it.

By trying to save it, you will condemn yourself.

Thinking with your present self

We do not want to change. Our present self does not want to change. Of course, it doesn't: if it did, we would be a different self, and our present self does not like another self because it only likes itself. If it *really* liked another self, it would already have become another self. If it didn't become another self, it is because it does not want to adapt or let go of any mental pattern it would have to.

Each mental pattern is both the decision-maker and the object of the decision to be let go, and therefore, *of course*, it votes for itself to stay.

Changing is a vote against our present self, and our present self would never vote against itself. Hence, the solution cannot be thinking with our present self.

Your future self (the person you will be after you adapt) thinks differently. Your future self is happy that the ineffective mental pattern was abandoned and that you adopted a more effective one instead.

Realizing that after a change, you will judge the change differently than you did before is a key enabler for personal change.

Let your future self make the decisions and lead your current self toward it.

Proposed exercises

- Some people benefit from visual processes such as writing down an old habit or facet of your personality on a piece of paper and then burning it to symbolize letting it go.

- Others benefit from mental processes such as meditating on the mental pattern to be let go and asking questions such as:

- Did it do any good for your life?

- Has its net impact on your life been positive or negative?

- Would the ideal person you wish to become benefit from that pattern?

Chapter summary

- Let go of the patterns that are preventing you from achieving what you could achieve.

- Do not think like your present self; think like your future self.

Further readings

The appendix essay *"Ego and Decision Making"* contains more information on the duality of present self / future self and on how our ego influences our decision-making.

1. Written by the @Gecorius_ on Twitter.

CONCLUSIONS

In the first part of the book, we saw that in an ever-changing world, adaptation is a necessity. There are only two possibilities: adaptation of the population as the unfit are excluded, or the suffering of the whole population (both the fit and the unfit). Subsequently, we explored how "exclusion of the unfit" can both apply to the unfit individuals within a population but also to the *unfit mental patterns* within an individual. Furthermore, it was illustrated that the removal of unfit mental patterns within individuals should be bottom-up (self-directed) so that its benefits can be longstanding.

In the second part of the book, we covered a 4-step method to achieve bottom-up, self-directed personal growth:

1. **Recognize the need** (for personal change)

2. **Host a multitude** (of mental patterns)

3. **Expose yourself** (to non-fatal harm, avoiding fatal one)

4. **Let go** (of those mental patterns of yours that proved unconducive to leading indicators)

The ideas in this book have had a very large impact on me, paving the way for my growth from an insecure school child to becoming a self-reliant man, an expert in his field, and helpful to others. I hope it might become equally important to you.

If you have any comments or questions, do not hesitate to write me at **Luca@luca-dellanna.com**

ABOUT THE AUTHOR
LUCA DELLANNA

An automotive engineer by training, after having led large teams and consulted for large multinationals, Luca quit his corporate job to become an independent researcher and author and dedicate his career to shedding light on the topic of emerging behavior.

After having lived in Spain, Germany, and Singapore, Luca recently moved back to his hometown of Turin (Italy). He spends his days between consulting, teaching, and conducting his research from his home, a coffee bar, or a park.

A few days a month, Luca also consults corporations and individuals that want to improve their businesses. Once per year, he teaches a Risk Management module at Genoa University, and a few times a year, he holds private intensive courses for entrepreneurs, operations managers, plant managers, and CEOs / COOs.

Luca writes regularly on Twitter (**@DellAnnaLuca**). You can visit his professional website and blog at **Luca-dellanna.com**. You can also contact him at **Luca@luca-dellanna.com** *(he reads all emails personally and usually replies within 48 hours)*.

In the following few pages, you can read a brief overview of Luca's other books. You can support Luca by recommending this book to your friends or colleagues and leaving a review on Amazon.

𝕏 x.com/DellAnnaLuca
 linkedin.com/in/dellannaluca
 youtube.com/LucaDellannaChannel

ALSO BY LUCA DELLANNA

Winning Long-Term Games

The key to winning long-term games is to stop playing them as a succession of *separate* short-term games.

Yet, most people take the opposite approach. Here are three examples:

- The manager who sees each interaction with her team as a *separate* game. Every time she talks to her subordinates, it's to get things done rather than develop their skills. As a result, she fails to build the long-term assets (a competent team) she needs in order to win her long-term game (a successful career).

- The spouse who lies to avoid responsibility. If lying has, say, a 1% chance of being discovered, it is a great short-term tactic (it succeeds 99% of the time) but a terrible long-term strategy (if you lie once a week, you have a 99.5% chance of getting caught over a decade).

- The solopreneur who sends weekly emails to their mailing list and sees each as a *separate* game. They *consume* their audience's trust to generate more sales within a single email instead of *building* trust to create more sales within a few months.

These three examples show that approaching long-term games as a succession of *separate* short-term games is a bad strategy *despite working great over short time horizons.*

In "Winning Long-Term Games," Luca guides the reader into designing strategies that not only have a long-term horizon but also *leverage the long term* to gain an edge against anyone with shorter time horizons and make success all but inevitable.

Winning Long-Term Games is planned to be published in the first half of 2024.

Ergodicity: How Irreversible Outcomes Affect Long-term Performance in Work, Investing, Relationships, Sport, and Beyond (3rd ed.)

"This is one of the most important books I've read, period. It's short, articulate, and expansive on a singular subject matter — ergodicity, which is really the key ingredient to success in life, marriage, business, family, happiness, health, etc."

— BLAKE JANOVER, JANOVER INC. CEO

"A great book for those who quickly want to familiarize themselves with the concept of ergodicity. The author goes to great lengths to explain the concept in easily understandable terms. Highly recommended!"

— AUKE HUNNEMAN

Best Practices for Operational Excellence (3ʳᵈ ed.)

"I'm a huge fan of High Output Management and Setting the Table [...] Luca's Best Practices for Operational Excellence took my management to the next level. It's been almost a month since I started implementing the principles, but I can already say that I've noticed a significant improvement in my company's morale [...] That feels amazing."

— *MOLSON HART, VIAHART CEO*

The Control Heuristic: The Nature of Human Behavior (2ⁿᵈ ed.)

"This book is like a magnificent suspension bridge, linking the science of the human brain to the practical craft of applying it in everyday life. I loved it."

— RORY SUTHERLAND

"A SUPERB book [...] by one of the profound thinkers in our field [behavioral economics]."

— MICHAL G. BARTLETT

"Luca's book was so helpful to my work. Opened my eyes up to some more reasons why change is so hard."

— CHRIS MURMAN

Managing Hybrid and Remote Teams (2nd ed.)

"Lots of specific and practical advice! Even experienced managers should find each chapter hugely valuable for reassessing their performance in each of the areas.

— *GABY LLOYD*

"Packed full of useful information. Luca takes the maddeningly difficult subject of managing a team and breaks it down into actionable activities. The sections on Clarity and Feedback are particularly strong, providing a way of viewing management as a nurturing and human activity.

— *DANIEL WEBB*

"Thought-provoking."

— *CARL BROWN*

100 Truths You Will Learn Too Late (3rd ed.)

"I am amazed at Luca Dellanna's ability to observe, compile, and articulate 99 very actionable life principles here. Each chapter describes the rule in a way that makes you think and then summarizes the Action. It's filled with DEEP insights yet VERY readable."

— *THERESIA TANZIL*

"Absolutely brilliant. You might have grasped some of these concepts before, but having them structured and in writing makes all the difference [...] I will surely recommend it to friends and co-workers."

— *ALBERTO PISANELLO*

"A very thoughtful piece of writing, deep and wiring!"

— *DAVID KREJCA*

The World Through a Magnifying Glass

"Thank you for helping me understand! My son was recently diagnosed, and I needed to be able to understand how he views the world. Why would certain things overwhelm him and cause so much anxiety and pain. This book made it so clear and easy to understand."

— *GEIGER T.*

Probably one of the best works I have read on autism (I have read a few), and it's surprising how realistically he depicts the condition."

— *MANEL VILAR*

"Loved The World Through a Magnifying Glass – this analogy NAILS IT."

— *EMERSON SPARTZ, NYT BESTSELLER AUTHOR*

APPENDIX

The appendix contains some essays of mine which did not fit the main topic of this book but might be relevant nevertheless. The essays are the following:

- **"Ego and decision making,"** on our ego's influence on decision-making and strategies for preventing it.
- **"New metrics for stability,"** on new metrics to measure long-term stability.
- **"The Antifragile Range,"** on how antifragile entities can exhibit fragile behavior and how to minimize the chances that they do. This content builds on Nassim Nicholas Taleb's book *Antifragile*, explaining the conditions that cause antifragile identities to behave as such and adding a dynamic analysis of the behavior of antifragile entities.

These are revisited versions of essays already published on my website, where you can find many more essays on several topics, the most frequent of which is human behavior and second-order effects: Luca-Dellanna.com

EGO AND DECISION-MAKING

There is no difference between ego investment and addiction: in both cases, we outsource decision-making to what has been good to us in the past.

That which we believe is important to us, is the criteria we use for making decisions.

Our ego is the sum of the entities to which we have outsourced our decision-making.

Therefore, where our ego is invested determines who will benefit from our actions.

Some examples:

- If our ego is invested in things, we will make decisions that benefit these things (and their producers), not decisions that benefit ourselves.

- If our ego is invested in people, we will make decisions that benefit these people. Moreover, they will only benefit from our decisions in the short term: our friends, families, and partners have more to gain from a version of ourselves who reached our own potential rather than a hollow version of ourselves whose development got compromised by our "selfless" actions.

- If our ego is invested in our membership in social groups, we will make decisions that benefit our membership, not ourselves. Moreover, we will end up empty-handed if, in the future, the group proves worse than we used to believe or if its attitude towards us changes.

- If our ego is invested in our present self, we will make short-term decisions that will ephemerally fulfill our present self but will prevent a solid foundation for our future self.

- **If, instead, our ego is invested in our future self, then we will make long-term decisions. Moreover, we will not suffer from present outcomes, as they are not final; we will only care about our long-term growth.** (Outcome is a lagging indicator; personal growth, a leading one. Using lagging indicators as bases for judgment always leads to bad decisions; using leading indicators, to good ones.)

Investing our ego in our future self is the only way out of addictions (towards things, people, and identities).

Investing our ego in our future self is the only way to ensure our long-term development and happiness.

NEW METRICS FOR STABILITY

The old saying goes: "What gets measured gets improved." Therefore, **we better choose the right metrics; otherwise, we end up adapting in a direction that is not good for us.** Many of the metrics we are usually primed for, such as quarterly sales or current salary, are similarly flawed and might direct their adopters towards acting against their long-term interests. In this chapter, we will look at some metrics which, if optimized, will reward us with a stable life.

———

Earthquakes are bound to happen. Oversimplifying, continents slide on plates floating on hot molten rock. Ideally, the plates would slide against each other frictionless; in practice, attrition causes them to grind against each other and temporarily stop in place, accumulating potential energy by elastically compressing themselves until they suddenly slide against each other, liberating the potential energy and causing the earthquake. Earthquakes are releases of potential energy. If such releases took place every day, we would mostly have many tiny daily earthquakes; instead, as potential energy is allowed to build up, devastating consequences accompany its rare, abrupt release.

Just like the plates shift slowly but constantly, inexorably shaping the continents we live on, every day, the environment changes and distances itself from the environment that was in the past. **Due to the constant change of the environment, every day that passes, what was fit in the past becomes increasingly unfit for the future – unless it adapts,** of course. Every day that passes without adaptation, potential energy builds up, threatening to produce increasing harm when its release comes.[1]

Before we dive into some metrics which, if optimized, will reward us with a stable life, we have to face a paradox: a truly stable life does not look stable at all. More precisely, a life that is **stable over the long term does not look stable in the short term.** Frequent, small adjustments are required on a regular basis in order to avoid abrupt, painful changes later on. A life that does not change for years is prone to suddenly become very unstable when the gap between what was required by the environment of the past and what is required by the environment in the present suddenly materializes, and change becomes inevitable.

The pain of change comes from resisting it. A log that hangs on the side of the river will be hurt by the continuous attrition and collisions with the water molecules flowing, whereas a log that goes with the flow will notice that the water molecules that touch it are almost still from its point of view.

Short-term stability is a predictor of long-term instability, and short-term instability is a prerequisite for long-term stability. The absence of harm today (so, no adaptation) is a predictor for harm tomorrow (when the need for adaptation will become unavoidable). Therefore, preventing pain is never a good argument for refraining from change, for it only delays the change and increases the inevitable pain.

Long-term stability is preceded by short-term change and, therefore, adaptation. Therefore, **the key to a stable future is to use**

adaptation-centric metrics instead of using metrics that focus on short-term stability. The more we adapt today, the more stable our future will be.

Adaptation as the metric to optimize for

Following the case made in the previous section, the presence of adaptation should be **the metric to optimize** – in particular, **adaptation to the full risk profile of the environment.**

One way to measure adaptation would be to do it directly: comparing yourself of today to yourself of last year and looking for changes (for adaptation causes changes). If you didn't change, chances are you should have, because your environment surely did change. However, some good judgment has to be used: the fact that one changed does not guarantee alone that he changed for the better.

Another way to measure adaptation is to do so indirectly: if someone got harmed (by good harm, as defined in Chapter 8) and survived, he probably also adapted. Harm could be a good proxy for adaptation,[2] *provided it is good harm*, though this can be challenging to achieve.

A solution comes from internalizing that we only suffer from what we do not adapt to, and we adapt to everything we get exposed to. Following this line of thought, **a good proxy for adaptation is the absence of barriers preventing the environment from harming us and, therefore, from triggering our adaptation** in the right direction. If barriers are absent, then the chances are that we are exposed to the environment and, therefore, adapting to it. Barriers are anything that is not part of ourselves and which prevents us from being hurt: for example, dams, a car's ABS, some excessively protective governmental policies, overly protective parents, excessive political correctness, and so on.

However, if we removed all barriers completely, the environment would seriously harm us. **The key is to remove the barriers that prevent light harm and keep those that prevent fatal harm.**

The justification for the previous two paragraphs is quite technical; the reader interested in it might want to read the appendix essay named *"The Antifragile Range."*

Exposure to the full risk profile

The environment comprises many threats. A tempting way to defend ourselves is to avoid some of them rather than addressing them or becoming stronger. As a result, we might end up being exposed to only some of the threats: a subset of the full risk profile of the environment. However, it is necessary to ensure that we are exposed to the full risk profile. If we were exposed to only a subset of the full environmental risk profile, we would adapt towards being less vulnerable to the threats in the subset and towards being *more* vulnerable to those threats that are not in the subset.

The fragile is just as adapted to the environment as the antifragile; but it only adapted to a subset of it. Unfortunately, it seems that the easiest way to make something *appear* to be fit for the environment is to reduce the scope of what the environment is. The easiest way to turn a dangerous building into a safe one is to assume that no earthquake will take place; the easiest way to turn a risky investment into a risk-free one is to assume that some negative events cannot happen or to say that the investment is risk-free in a confidence interval; the easiest way to make a theory solid is to add an assumption.

Each time a person refuses to expose herself to the full risk profile of the environment, she will adapt towards being more vulnerable to the parts of it she did not expose herself to. She is then likely to adopt a survival strategy consisting of doing her best not to expose herself outside of the small, comfortable subset of the environment she decided to live in. Soon, most of her energies will have to be dedicated to keeping herself insulated from the real, outside world. Conversely, the more you expose yourself to the full risk profile, the less you will have to worry about what you get exposed to, therefore becoming able to enjoy unprecedented freedom.

Skin in the game

Skin in the game (the property of being harmed if one's own actions or suggestions end up being wrong) is another strong predictor of adaptation. Nassim Nicholas Taleb wrote an excellent, homonymous book on the concept.

For what concerns the matters at hand here, **skin in the game ensures harm when one's own actions end up being wrong. By guaranteeing harm, it guarantees adaptation.**

Moreover, because it makes the risks of contemplated actions more real, it generally also ensures the safety of adaptation: if someone has skin in the game, he is less likely to take fatal risks, unless they are necessary.

As Nassim Nicholas Taleb wrote,[3] "Skin in the game has the attribute of removing bad drivers from the system. Systems learn by removing". In the context of this book, I could adapt his sentence as "Skin in the game has the attribute of removing bad mental patterns from the system. Systems, and people, learn by removing".

Decentralization

Decentralization is another helpful proxy for adaptation. The more a system is decentralized, the more it can be exposed to risks and survive: in case of harm, only a portion of the system would risk game-over, and the rest could learn from it.

Companies can decentralize by diversifying their business, sourcing a given input from multiple suppliers, and ensuring that key roles have a ready backup. Examples of how individuals can decentralize are the object of Chapter 13.

Metrics for personal stability

Some examples of metrics for personal stability.

- **Time and resources spent solving the sources of problems rather than avoiding them:** as seen in Chapter 8, solving the sources of problems causes us to encounter fewer problems and, therefore, to live a more stable life.[4]

- **"Talks" vs. "Walks":** sometimes we "talk" (we say what we should or will do), and sometimes we "walk" (we actually *do* what we say we should or will do). Only the latter exposes us to harm from our actions and, therefore, to the possibility of adaptation.

- **The ability to "decentralize yourself".** This is explained in Chapter 13.

Chapter summary

- Long-term stability is not preceded by the absence of volatility but by the presence of adaptation.

- Three metrics predict long-term stability:

- Adaptation to the full risk profile of the environment.

- Absence of barriers & presence of skin in the game.

- Decentralization.

---

1. Unless the environment reverses its direction of change so that it becomes more similar to what it was. However, this is seldom the case.

2. The idea that exposing yourself to good harm necessarily corresponds to adaptation is not new. Many advocate that building good habits and systems allows you to proceed in the right direction and build skills and competencies even if individual projects fail until eventually you become so good that success – however you define it – will follow.

3. Twitter, 23rd of September 2018.

4. Wait! Aren't problems good, because they are sources of harm? In general, yes. However, **facing the same problems over and over again means that there is harm without adaptation** – for if we adapted, we would be able to face and resolve the *source* of the problems. Facing the same problem over and over is useless and a symptom of avoiding adaptation.

THE ANTIFRAGILE RANGE

This essay assumes familiarity with the concept of Antifragile, *which is explained in Nassim Nicholas Taleb's homonymous book. If you are not familiar with the concept, please read the following footnote, as it will be helpful.*[1]

―――――

Antifragility is the capacity to benefit from stressors. For example, we humans are antifragile: by lifting weights (and therefore applying stress to our muscles), we become stronger. Yet, they can break, such as their ankle, if they jump from too high. **Antifragile beings only benefit from a given range of stressors.** Moreover, antifragile beings can become weaker, such as my grandma aging. Antifragile things can *appear to* become fragile with time. They never actually lose antifragility (the capacity to benefit from some stressors); rather, the range of stressors that are beneficial for them shrinks. **Though antifragile entities never become fragile, they might change the range of stressors in reaction to which they express an antifragile behavior.**

Type	Stressors they like	Stressors they dislike
Fragile beings	None	All
Antifragile beings	Those in a range	Those outside the range

In this essay, **we will explore the conditions upon which antifragile entities might change their response profile to stressors – a process that I call fragilization** (or antifragilization, depending on the direction of the shift of the range of stressors that benefits them).

In particular, I will first demonstrate three points:

- **Whether an antifragile entity reacts to a stressor by exhibiting an antifragile behavior (becoming stronger) or by exhibiting a fragile behavior (breaking) depends not only on the stressor but on whether the stressor causes distributed harm to the antifragile entity,** a condition that is influenced by the robustness of the antifragile entity itself and by other characteristics of its.

- **Such reactions to stressors change the robustness of the antifragile entity and, therefore influence the future likelihood that it will react differently to future stressors.**

- Therefore, the study of the second-order[2] effects on antifragility is just as important as that of first-order effects (if not more important, in the long term).

Finally, I will provide **an analysis of such second-order effects.**

Antifragile entities can exhibit fragile behavior

Humans are antifragile. The mechanical stress of repeatedly jumping over a moderate obstacle makes their leg muscles and joints stronger: an antifragile behavior. However, jumping from 5 meters tends to instead break their legs: a fragile behavior. It turns out that antifragile entities exhibit antifragile behavior only to a limited range of stressors. If the stressor is extremely high, even an antifragile entity will break. If a stressor is too low (such as lifting a matchbox), no benefit at all will take place. Therefore, whether an antifragile entity exhibits a fragile or antifragile behavior depends also on the strength of the stressor stressing it. Antifragile response is closely tied to a range of stressors, with a minimum threshold and a maximum one.[3]

The difference between antifragile and fragile entities is not that the former do not break under stressors. Rather, antifragile entities have a range of stressors towards which they react by becoming stronger. Moreover, antifragile entities are adaptive, and fragile ones are not.

In the rest of this essay, we will examine further how antifragile entities adapt to their environment.[4]

Antifragile entities cannot become fragile (i.e., they never fully lose the property to react to some stressors positively). Instead, the range of stressors that cause a positive reaction in them can shrink. I call *fragilization* such a reduction in range, and *antifragilization* the opposite shift (an increase).

Before delving into the details, one example: take Marco, a guy who recently started at my gym and currently deadlifts 250 pounds. He can easily lift 150 pounds; however, doing so does not do much to grow his muscles. If he were to try to lift 350 pounds, he would injure himself. Too little, no gain; too much, and pain. His sweet spot to entice the maximum antifragile response is currently about 250 pounds. If Marco keeps training, he can gain strength up to the point where he is able to lift 350 pounds. At that point, it would take 400 pounds to injure him. If he lifts 350, he gains muscle. By lifting weights over time, Marco managed to enlarge the range of stressors that are beneficial to him. He antifragilized. Conversely, were he to stop training for a few years, he would lose the capacity to deadlift 250 pounds. After five years, he might be able to deadlift only 200 pounds. Trying to deadlift 250 could injure him. The range of weights that he can use to strengthen himself safely has now shrunk. Marco fragilized. The chart below depicts what happens to Marco when he antifragilized: the light-gray range of stressors (the one where his body benefits from lifting) got larger.

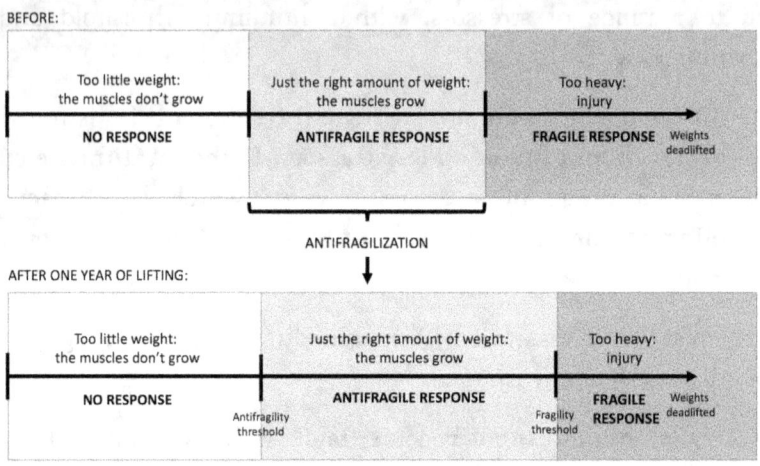

The conditions for antifragility

Antifragile entities have a common property: they comprise a population of sub-entities at a lower layer. Some examples:

- Animals and plants are composed of cells.
- Species are composed of a population of animals or plants.

However, even though ceramic vases are composed of a population of ceramic molecules, they are fragile. Something is missing in the previous definition. Let's be more specific:

Antifragile entities have a common property: they comprise, at a lower level, a population of sub-entities *that can be subject to harm.* Some examples:

- Animals and plants are composed of cells; if subject to a stressor, the weakest cells die.

- Species are composed of a population of animals or plants; if subject to a stressor, the weakest members die.

Harm is what facilitates antifragility. Harm necessitates stressors (to harm the weakest).

You might say: "Hey, the molecules of a ceramic vase also undergo harm: if you make a vase fall, some of the molecules that form it (or rather, some of the bonds between them) will break; moreover, it's not random ones that break: it's the weakest ones." Something is missing, again.

Antifragile entities only exhibit antifragile behavior when their underlying population is harmed *in a distributed way*. Let's re-examine the examples from above:

- Animals are composed of cells; if subject to a stressor, the weakest cells are harmed. If the weakest cells that get harmed are distributed, the exhibited behavior is antifragile (lifting weights at the gym only tears a few muscle fibers here and there, and the muscles regrow them in excess, becoming stronger). If the weakest cells that get harmed are concentrated, the exhibited behavior is fragile (if I lift a very heavy high, my muscle might strain, and I lose the ability to use it properly for a few days; if I jump from the third floor, all the cells in a given area of my leg bone break and the bone breaks).

- Species are composed of a population of animals or plants; if subject to a stressor (such as famine), the weakest members die. If the members die in a distributed way (some members of this tribe, some children of this family), then the tribe or family grows stronger (thanks to natural selection and learning): an antifragile behavior. However, if all the members of a local population die, then, simply, that tribe is exterminated without opportunity for adaptation (through natural selection): a fragile behavior.

We now see that **another necessary property of antifragile entities is the ability to regrow new members of the population it comprises** (either in number or in size) (and regrow them in a quantity that is higher than the one needed to survive their current environment).[5]

The reduction of stressors range enticing antifragile responses

In the previous part, I described how an entity needs four conditions to be able to express an antifragile behavior; in other words, to be adaptive:

- To be composed of a population at a lower layer,
- To allow for natural selection to act (more on this later),
- To ensure that any harm inflicted affects its lower layer in a distributed way,
- To be able to grow their lower-layer population up to the point of redundancy.

Now, let's explore what happens if natural selection is prevented (through the removal of skin in the game, i.e., by insulating the actor from the consequences of his actions, or through the introduction of "fences,"[6] i.e., protection measures insulating a population from stressors) and what happens if conditions are present, which might cause its population to be harmed in a non-distributed way. As we will see, in both cases, the consequence is fragility.

First, let's see how a fragile entity reacts to stressors.

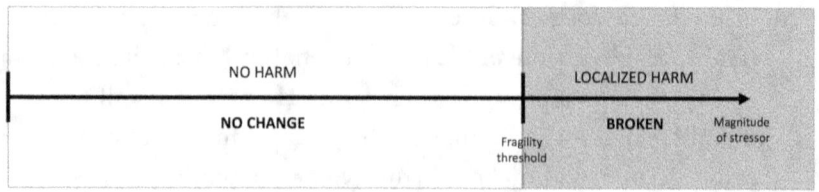

If the intensity of the stressor is lower than the fragility threshold, no change happens (if I let a ceramic vase fall from 1 inch, it doesn't break).

If the intensity of the stressor is higher than the fragility threshold, the fragile entity breaks because its lower-layer population incurs localized damage (if I let a ceramic vase fall from 3 feet, the molecule bonds along a weak crystal boundary break, and a crack appears).

(Note that for the purpose of explaining the current concepts, we are considering single stressors only. Some entities exhibit a behavior called "fatigue failure," where the effects of smaller stressors accrue over time.)

Now, let's see how an antifragile entity reacts to stressors.

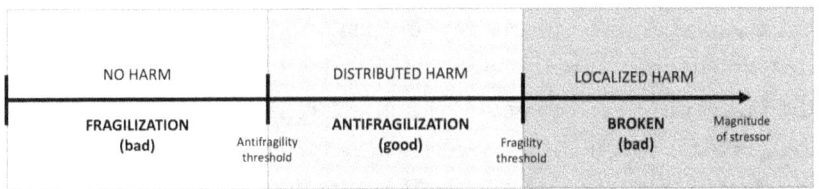

If the intensity of the stressor is higher than the fragility threshold, the antifragile entity breaks because some of its lower-layer population is harmed *in a localized pattern* (for example, if I jump from the second floor, I might break a bone: a few cells break along a line in my bone).

If the intensity of the stressor is between the fragility threshold and the antifragility threshold (respectively, the left and the right border of the light gray area above), then *antifragilization* happens. For example, if I jump fifty times over a 2-foot-tall obstacle, I will grow some leg muscles. Antifragilization happens because the lower-layer population is harmed *in a distributed way* (for example, if I break some muscle fibers here and there: this triggers muscle regrowth. If I exercise too hard, I will tear the muscle fibers in a localized way and suffer a muscle strain: an injury). I call this behavior antifragilization because it modifies the future response of an antifragile entity to future stressors. Following the effect of the stressor in the antifragilization area, the fragility threshold shifts to the right (as displayed in the image on the next page) as the entity grows stronger and is able to withstand more intense stressors without breaking (the more I go to the gym, the more I can lift without straining myself). As a result, there is a larger proportion of stressors that induce an antifragile response in my entity: I became more antifragile. Hence, antifragilization.

If the intensity of the stressor is, instead, lower than the antifragility threshold (the right border of the white area in the image above), then no member of the lower-layer population is harmed. For example, if I lift a matchbox, the weight is too low to break any of my muscle fibers and induce any muscle growth. **If, over time, no stressor happens to be higher than the antifragility threshold, then *fragilization* happens.** If I do not exercise for a few months, my muscle mass will decrease, and I will reduce my ability to lift heavy weights. In this case, both the antifragility threshold and the fragility one decrease (shifting to the left in the image above). Because the fragility threshold is lowered, the antifragile entity is now more likely to express a fragile behavior (because, given a stable distribution of stressors, now a bigger proportion of them falls above such threshold). Therefore, fragilization. I will describe this behavior over the next paragraphs, just after antifragilization.

Antifragilization

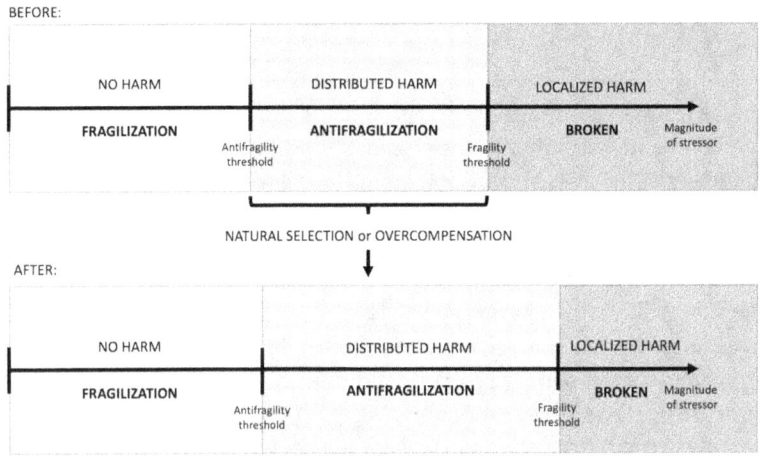

As displayed in the image above, **antifragilization** (the process that happens when an antifragile entity is exposed to stressors whose intensity falls between the fragility and antifragility thresholds) **consists of distributed harm, followed by an adaptation and subsequent increase in both the antifragility and the fragility threshold, and in the range of stressors causing an antifragile response** (the light gray portion of the axis). The increase in the fragility threshold is bigger than the increase in the antifragility threshold; therefore, the range of stressors inducing an antifragile reaction is bigger, and therefore, the antifragile entity becomes more likely to exhibit an antifragile reaction.

Antifragilization is the result of adaptation following distributed harm. On the next page, I will show a step-by-step example.

Step	Example
1) A stressor hits the antifragile entity.	For example, I lift some weights.
2) The stressor is strong enough to produce some harm: it kills the weakest members of the lower-level population.	Lifting the weights causes some of my muscle fibers to break.
3) In antifragile entities, those weakest members are usually distributed; therefore, distributed harm occurs. The distributed harm is well-absorbed by the entity and therefore does not cause it to permanently lose any functionality.	The muscle fibers which break are not grouped in a single location (as it would happen in case of a strain) but are distributed along all the muscle.
4) A first effect is that in organisms, the survivors who are left to reproduce are stronger than the average of the population before the harm, therefore the average of the next generation will be stronger. In organs, the tissue which breaks is repaired in a way that makes it stronger than it was (overcompensation). As a second effect, the intense stressor creates an expectation of more intense stressors to come, so the need for redundancy is established, and overgrowth/overcompensation is triggered.	Lifting weights creates the expectation, in my body, that it will have to lift more weights in the future; it should prepare itself for the task by growing muscles which are not only strong enough to lift the weight I just lifted, but even stronger to lift even heavier weights.
5) The consequence of the two effects described before is an increased tolerance to stressors, which causes both the antifragility and the fragility thresholds to increase.	Now, I can lift heavier weights without suffering injuries, but must also lift heavier weights if I want to further grow my muscles.

Fragilization

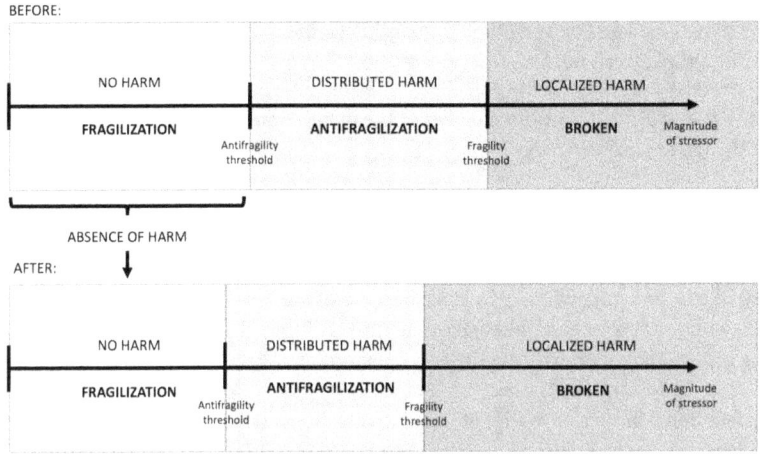

In the diagram above, both the antifragility threshold and the fragility threshold reduce (they move to the left along the axis indicating the magnitude of stressors), and the range of stressors eliciting an antifragile response shrinks (the light gray area).

Fragilization is the result of the lack of stressors and, thus, of harm.

Step by step:

Step	Example
1) Let's take the example of an antifragile entity which for some time lacks exposure to stressors above the antifragility threshold.	For example, for three months I do not make any physical exercise.
2) In that period of time, no member of the population at the lower layer is harmed.	In those three months, no muscle fiber tears because of an applied physical stressor.
3) A first effect takes place, which differs between organisms and organs. In organisms, because of the lack of natural selection, the weakest members of the lower-layer population do not die and are therefore allowed to reproduce. The second-generation population will thus have a lot of weak members. In organs, no damage reparation takes place to offset decay; therefore, the tissue shrinks.	No muscle fiber broke, therefore no healing process is triggered which would cause reconstruction. The fibers are left to decay and become weaker.
4) A second effect takes place: because of the lack of stressors, there is no (apparent) need for redundancy anymore. Redundancy is useful only in bad times; in good ones, it seems unnecessary. Therefore, the antifragile entity adapts in such a way to reduce redundancy. This makes sense, because **optimization is an adaptation to stability** (for it assumes certain conditions, to which the entity optimizes for, to be present also in the future), whereas **redundancy is an adaptation to volatility** (for, if no condition is assumed stable, there is no stable condition to optimize for). The lack of redundancy makes the antifragile entity more vulnerable to failure, and therefore more fragile (the fragility threshold becomes lower).	Because I didn't lift any weight for months, my body assumes I will not have to lift any weight in the future either. It then appears advantageous to reduce the number of muscle cells (to save energy, between other reasons).
5) The consequence of the two effects described before is a decreased tolerance to stressors, which causes both the antifragility and the fragility thresholds to decrease.	The muscle loss makes me more likely to strain a muscle if I will suddenly have to lift a heavy weight.

The influence of environmental stability

As described with the two processes of fragilization and antifragilization, the range of stressors that induce an antifragile reaction in an antifragile entity is not fixed. Antifragile entities are adaptive: this confers them an advantage in a changing environment. They adapt in opposite directions to stable and unstable environments. **Adapting to an unstable environment makes an adaptive entity "more antifragile"** (i.e., more likely to exhibit an antifragile reaction and to adapt to its environment), **whereas adapting to a stable environment makes an adaptive entity "less antifragile"** (i.e., less likely to exhibit an antifragile reaction). Antifragile entities never lose their capacity to be adaptive (i.e., to benefit from stressors in a given range); however, they might shrink the range of stressors towards which they react adaptively. Therefore, **though antifragile entities never become fragile, they might change their likelihood to react to stressors by exhibiting fragile behavior.**

Whether a stressor will induce a fragile or antifragile response depends on both the magnitude of the stressor and the strength of the entity undergoing stress. Assuming the environmental *distribution* of stressors is constant, a change in strength directly corresponds to a change in the likelihood of a given distribution of stressors to induce a certain kind of response. For example, the stronger my ankles, the less likely I am to break my ankle when I step into a hole in the street.

The importance of distributed harm

As can be seen in the examples above, **a lack of distributed harm causes fragilization.** To increase the likelihood of an antifragile response, it is necessary to preserve a condition of susceptibility to distributed harm (implementing the advice at the core of this book).

In particular, **hacks and quick fixes, which aim to bypass distributed harm by offering apparently safer shortcuts, actually bring fragility.**

There are two processes that prevent harm: the removal of skin in the game and the introduction of exogenous barriers (aka "fences")[7]. The next part of this essay will describe them, clarifying why they are dangerous and why they should be avoided.

Introduction of skin in the game

One is said to have "skin in the game" if he is directly affected by the outcome of an event in both a positive and a negative way. At the core of this book, we already saw how, for example, a biker has skin in the game of his driving – if he is subject to an incident, he is likely to get injured. A trader in a bank instead does not have skin in the game: if his investments go well, both he and the bank receive huge bonuses; however, if his investments perform badly, the bank is set to lose a lot of money, but the trader does not have to pay any maluses.

First, let's see what happens if skin in the game is increased in the population forming the lower layer of the antifragile entity. For example, if a country (an antifragile entity) passes a law to enforce skin in the game for its citizens (the population at the lower layer).

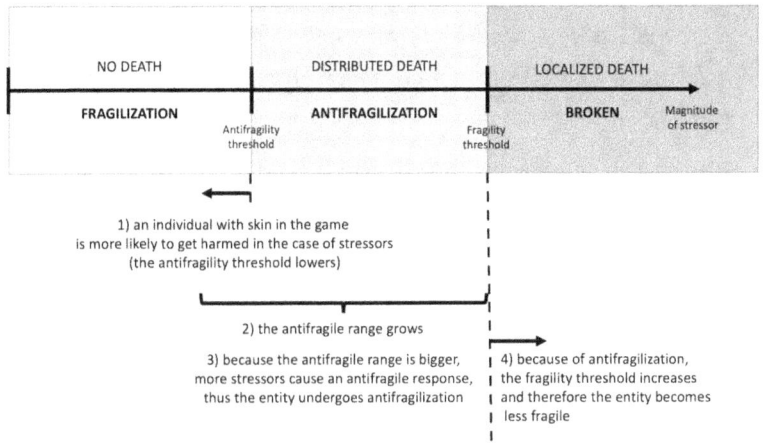

1. First, the introduction of skin in the game promotes direct accountability. One is more likely to suffer for his mistakes. The more skin in the game, the more, *as a first-order effect*, individuals are likely to be harmed in case of stressors; such failure is likely to be distributed (thanks to skin in the game, only the weak individuals fail, without bringing anyone down with them). Therefore, it is the antifragility threshold that gets lowered (a lower antifragile threshold is an indicator that a given stressor distribution is more likely to cause harm). *For example, a bank decides to cause traders to get both bonuses* and *maluses based on the performance of their investments. Now, a market downturn is more likely to hurt some of the traders.*

2. Because the antifragility threshold is lowered, the antifragilization range (the light gray area) grows bigger.

3. A random stressor is now more likely to induce antifragilization (a stressor that would have hit the right side of the white area would now hit the left side of the light gray area). Therefore, antifragilization is more likely to happen. *Because a market downturn is more likely to hurt some of the*

traders, eventually causing the less performing ones to lose their jobs, the bank is more likely to benefit from a downturn in the measure it removes the bad traders from its trading division, leaving the good ones only.

4. As a result of antifragilization, the fragility threshold increases. Now, a random stressor from a given stressor distribution is more likely to hit the antifragilization area (a stressor that would have hit the dark gray area on its left side would now hit the light gray area on its right side: the boundary between them has shifted to the right). The entity is now more likely to exhibit an antifragility response. *As a result of a financial downturn, the traders whose investments performed the worst lost their jobs. The bank now mostly contains good traders.*

5. Because of the antifragile response being solicited more often, antifragilization also happens more often, and the fragility threshold now increases moving to the right, offsetting the movement it did to the left during the first step. *Because at the bank, only wiser traders are left, those traders, by virtue of being wiser, are less likely to be hurt during an eventual future downturn. The bank is now stronger than it was (its traders, and thus its investments, are better) and thus can withstand bigger financial downturns in the future.*

As a result, **thanks to skin in the game, all members of the population are now safer** (less likely to get hurt because of a random stressor).

First and second-order effects

It is worth noting that the dominant effect, and the only significant one over the long term, is the one described in the fifth point above: a second-order effect. First-order effects are those that depend on the immediate response of a population based on its current characteristics; second-order effects are those that depend on how the population changes its characteristics to better cope in the future with whatever caused the first-order effect. Because policymakers usually only think in terms of first-order effects, they might neglect second-order ones, ending up making wrong decisions that appear to work in the short term but do not achieve the desired long-term result.

Now, let's see what happens in the opposite case: the removal of skin in the game.

Introduction of exogenous barriers (aka, "fences") and the removal of skin in the game

In "The Fence Paradox," Italian professor Pasquale Cirillo tells a story of tourists taking pictures from the edge of a canyon. Since it is a risky endeavor, only a few tourists venture to the edge, and those who do so do it with great care. One day, one of them goes a bit too far on the edge and falls down, dying. In response to this unlucky event, a fence is built on the edge of the canyon. It now *looks* safe to take pics from the edge, and tourists flock in. They lean on the fence to take pictures and push each other in an attempt to take better shots. One day, a big group of tourists rely too much on the fence, and they apply too much of their weight to it by leaning over it to take better pictures: the fence collapses, causing the whole group to fall and die. After all, the fence didn't make the canyon safer; it only made it safer for the population exposed to (or exposing itself to) smaller stressors, whereas it made it less safe in case of exposure to bigger stressors (or making the population more likely to expose themselves to bigger stressors).

Because barriers prevent the smallest stressors from harming people, they feel safe and therefore invite them to take more risks, increasing the risk of an important negative event once a stronger stressor appears.

Humans do not like risky environments and often introduce barriers to make them safer. However, **often, such barriers only increase the sense of safety but decrease *actual* safety by inviting risk-taking.**

The image below describes the fragilization that follows the introduction of exogenous barriers. The attentive reader will notice that introducing exogenous barriers produces the opposite effect than increasing skin of the game, the topic of the previous section. This is because, indeed, introducing barriers removes the condition necessary for skin in the game (the possibility of being hurt), and removing barriers creates skin in the game. In other words, every time we introduce exogenous barriers and every time we reduce exogenous barriers, we introduce skin in the game.

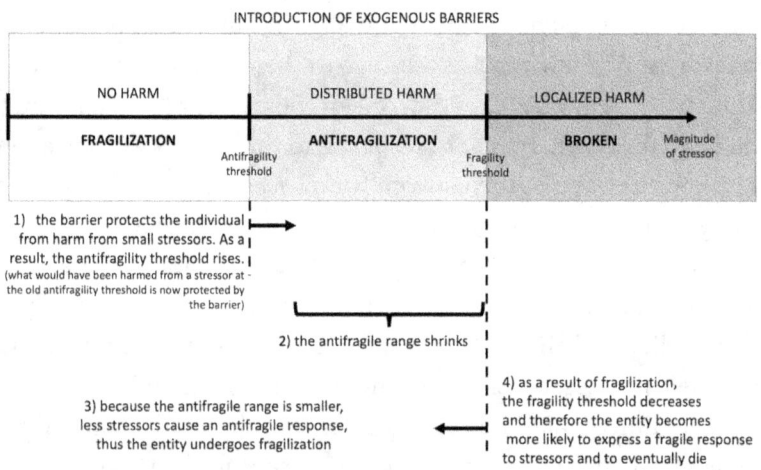

1. First, the introduction of exogenous barriers reduces direct accountability: one is less likely to suffer for his mistakes. *As a first-order effect*, weak individuals are less likely to fail in case of (small) stressors; therefore, the fragility threshold increases.

2. Because the antifragility threshold increases, the antifragilization range (the light gray area) becomes smaller.

3. A random stressor is now less likely to induce antifragilization (a stressor that would have hit the left side of the light gray area would now hit the right side of the white area). Therefore, antifragilization is less likely to happen, and fragilization is now more likely to take place.

4. As a result of fragilization, the fragility threshold decreases. As a consequence, a random stressor is now more likely to cause death (a stressor that would have hit the light gray area on its right side would now hit the dark gray area on its left side), and the entity is now more likely to exhibit a fragile response.

As a result, **thanks to the introduction of exogenous barriers, all members of the population are now less safe** (more likely to die in a localized way in case of exposure to a strong stressor).

The impact of redundancy on fragilization

In risk management, redundancy is defined as "having more than needed of something," and, unlike in corporate jobs where it is synonymous with layoffs, it is very important. For example, humans have two kidneys, even though they could live very well with a single one. That does not mean that the redundant kidney is useless – it is useless *when things go well.* When things go wrong – for example, a kidney failure – then suddenly, the redundant items become an asset that might make the difference between life and death.

No one considers a fire extinguisher redundant – no one says, "I wish I didn't buy the fire extinguisher" if their house did not take fire for a few years. In other fields, people – especially people without skin in the game – become quite averse to redundancy and see it as a cost to be minimized. Considering this, let's now explore the impact of redundancy on fragilization.

On a first-order analysis, redundancy might seem to reduce the likelihood of antifragilization, for there is a higher probability that an exterior stressor does not cause harm. For example, if I am strong (i.e., I have redundant muscles for most daily activities), I will not grow muscles by lifting my not-too-heavy grocery bags, whereas if I am weak and start lifting heavy grocery bags every day, I might actually grow some muscles.

However, **a second-order analysis shows the opposite consequence: redundancy is one of the factors that increase one's willingness to expose oneself to stressors and/or his opportunities to do so.** A strong person is more likely to *voluntarily* expose herself to stressors (for example, stepping in during a fight). In contrast, a weak person is less likely to voluntarily expose herself to stressors (for example, offering to help to move furniture).

Moreover, a stronger person (i.e., a person with redundant muscles) is more likely to survive a stronger-than-usual stressor, meaning that he is more likely to survive and benefit from the stressors. A weak person (one with no redundancy) is more likely to injure themselves or to die in case of extreme physical stress and, therefore, less likely to continue their exposure to the smaller, more beneficial stressors that will take place in the future.

Therefore, a certain degree of redundancy is beneficial to antifragility.

How to antifragilize?

To conclude, there are four necessary conditions for antifragility and four actions that can increase it.

The four necessary conditions for an entity to be able to express an antifragile behavior:

- It must be composed of a population at a lower layer (hence, "Chapter 13: Host a Multitude"), and

- Harm must be allowed at that lower layer, and

- Harm must happen in a distributed fashion, and

- The surviving members of the population must be able to reproduce.

The four actions which can increase the likelihood of an antifragile response to a random stressor are:

- Ensuring skin in the game.
- Removing exogenous barriers (aka, fences).
- Creating redundancy.
- Reducing systemicity.

Before seeing how to apply those last 4 points to both your personal life and the eventual organization you might be part of, it is worth noting that the four action points above are all second-order effects (their primary component is an adaptation over time), and that understanding them requires a dynamic representation of the world which static models cannot capture.

Application to your personal life

Here are some examples of how the four actions described above could apply to your personal life:

- Ensuring skin in the game: do not ever make a prediction that you do not follow with money. For example, whenever you catch yourself saying to a friend that you really think that a stock will go up, buy it (not investment advice; trade carefully and never more than you can afford to lose). This will make sure that you will have to feel the consequences (did the stock actually increase in value) *and that you will learn from your mistakes.*

- Removing exogenous barriers (aka, fences): look for feedback and accept it as truthful rather than defending your actions. Do not protect yourself; let the feedback hurt you so that you can learn and improve. Better said: **let the feedback hurt the** mental pattern of yours that caused it so that you can let go of it.

- Creating redundancy: save a percentage of your salary; learn to do your job better than you have not to get fired.

- Reducing systemicity: ensure that your family's income does not rely on your good health only, so that you can afford to be ill or, more importantly, take career risks that might present a significant upside.

Application to your organization

Here are some examples of how the four actions described above could apply to your organization:

- Ensuring skin in the game, closely tying performance to results. Few things are more damaging than letting your people unaccountable for their actions (both positives and negatives). If they aren't accountable for them, they will never learn from their mistakes, and/or they will take selfish actions (such as not taking on a project that might be positive for the company but which might represent more work for them).

- Removing exogenous barriers (aka, fences): ensure that nothing stands in the way of feedback. Often, managers withhold feedback because they do not want to hurt or demotivate their employees, or because they feel uncomfortable having difficult conversations. Both are a symptom of an exogenous barrier (trying to prevent someone from feeling hurt).

- Creating redundancy: ensure that you have enough resources (employees, stock, bandwidth, money, etc.) and procedures in place to deal with breakdowns (such as bad weather causing supply chain disruption, flu epidemics, unexpected surges in orders, and so on). This way, you can transform a negative systemic event into opportunities (a flood causing supply chain disruption? Good news for you: while your competitors cannot produce because no supplier is delivering, you will be the only one with a stocked warehouse: a competitive advantage).

- Reducing systemicity: ensure that none of your processes rely on a single person or machine: they might be ill, the machine might break down, and so on. Again, this allows you to transform negative events affecting your local environment into opportunities (flu epidemic? While your competitors' operations are disrupted because a key manager there is ill, yours will be as smooth as ever).

How to become antifragile?

To conclude, there are four necessary conditions for antifragility and four actions that can increase it.

The four necessary conditions for an entity to be antifragile:

- It must be composed of a population at a lower layer, and
- Harm must be allowed at that lower layer, and
- Harm must take place in a distributed fashion, and
- The surviving members of the population must be able to reproduce/regrow.

The four actions that can increase the likelihood of an antifragile response to a random stressor:

- Ensuring skin in the game.
- Removing exogenous barriers (aka, fences).
- Encouraging redundancy.
- Reducing systemicity.

It is worth noting that the four action points above are all second-order effects and that understanding them requires a dynamic representation of the world. People using static models are unable to understand second-order effects and, therefore, are likely to dismiss them as useless.

Further readings

I published a few videos on antifragility and on how individuals and organizations can become more antifragile on my YouTube channel, youtube.com/c/LucaDellannaChannel

---

1. Humans and other living beings are antifragile: they benefit from stressors. Does it sound weird? Think about the last time you went to the gym: applying a physical stressor (the weights you lifted) made your muscles grow. Moreover, antifragile entities benefit from stressors in a nonlinear way. If you walk 2 kilometers per day, your athletic condition will not improve that much. However, if you run one kilometer per day at approximately twice your walking speed, your athletic condition will improve noticeably. The intensity of the stressor matters more than how many times it is applied. Other entities, such as ceramic vases, are **fragile: they are harmed by stressors, in a nonlinear way.** If you let a ceramic vase fall one hundred times from one inch, it will not break. However, if you let it fall once from one hundred inches, it will break.

2. First-order effects are those that take place before a population adapts; second-order effects are those that include the adaptation of a population to first-order effects and its behavior after that.

3. These thresholds are probabilistic. A given stressor has a certain percentage of inducing a response, and another percentage of inducing another response. For example, if I jump from the first floor, there is a probability of my ankle breaking. Such responses can usually be modeled with an S-function. As a simplification with the purpose of explaining the principle of fragilization more clearly, for the rest of the essay, I will consider such S-functions as step-functions instead.

4. Or rather, how antifragile entities adapt to the stressors profile of their environment.

5. This is needed because, otherwise, a stronger-than-usual stressor might kill the antifragile entity, preventing future adaptation (no one is left).

6. The term "fences" refers to Italian researcher Pasquale Cirillo's "Fence Paradox," which will be the object of one of the last sections of this essay.

7. I call them exogenous to differentiate them from barriers inherent to the population itself, such as a turtle's shell, which do not necessarily cause fragilization.

GLOSSARY

Adaptation: a process which induces a change in the members of a population, increasing its fitness.

Evolution: an adaptive process which changes the genes of the population undergoing it.

Fitness: the ability to survive the environment.

Mental pattern: a situation-response pattern, engrained in the brain of an individual. Examples are habits, feelings, reactions and decision-making patterns.

Natural selection: a key mechanism of evolution, which ensures that the genetic makeup of a species drifts in a direction such to overcompensate for whatever threats killed part of the previous generation.